T0193603

Humbling OURSELVES AT THE FEET OF Jesus

BEREA THOMAS

WESTBOW
PRESS®
A DIVISION OF THOMAS NELSON
& ZONDERVAN

WestBow Press books may be ordered through booksellers or by contacting:

WestBow Press
A Division of Thomas Nelson & Zondervan
1663 Liberty Drive
Bloomington, IN 47403
www.westbowpress.com
844-714-3454

Because of the dynamic nature of the Internet, any web addresses or links contained in this book may have changed since publication and may no longer be valid. The views expressed in this work are solely those of the author and do not necessarily reflect the views of the publisher, and the publisher hereby disclaims any responsibility for them.

Any people depicted in stock imagery provided by Getty Images are models, and such images are being used for illustrative purposes only.
Certain stock imagery © Getty Images.

Scripture quotations marked (ESV) are from the ESV® Bible (The Holy Bible, English Standard Version®), copyright © 2001 by Crossway, a publishing ministry of Good News Publishers. Used by permission. All rights reserved.

Scripture marked (KJV) taken from the King James Version of the Bible.

Scripture quotations marked (NIV) are taken from the Holy Bible, New International Version®, NIV®. Copyright © 1973, 1978, 1984, 2011 by Biblica, Inc.® Used by permission of Zondervan. All rights reserved worldwide. www. zondervan.com The "NIV" and "New International Version" are trademarks registered in the United States Patent and Trademark Office by Biblica, Inc.®

Scripture marked (NKJV) taken from the New King James Version®. Copyright © 1982 by Thomas Nelson. Used by permission. All rights reserved.

ISBN: 978-1-6642-3144-3 (sc)
ISBN: 978-1-6642-3143-6 (hc)
ISBN: 978-1-6642-3145-0 (e)

Library of Congress Control Number: 2021908140

Print information available on the last page.

WestBow Press rev. date: 05/13/2021

Contents

Dedication

I first and foremost want to give honor to my Lord and Savior Jesus Christ for putting in my spirit the idea for the pictures and the words that accompanied each visual art.

My children Brandon and Liana simply because I love you and I wanted to acknowledge you in this book.

I also want to thank my spiritual mom M.Ed., M.A.P.T., D.D. Linda Millsap-Jones. You have been instrumental to my overall soul with your teachings and guidance. I love you, honor you, and appreciate you dearly.

I want to conclude with giving thanks to Roberta for assisting me in proofreading this book. I dearly thank you from the bottom of my heart for helping a sista out!

You all are blessings to me.

Chapter 1
WHO'S IN CONTROL OF YOUR LIFE

My flesh loved being in control of my life. When I made decisions and planned my daily agenda, I was in charge. I was behind the cockpit steering my life and taking care of all the responsibilities that were in the cabin and cargo area in the airplane of my life. I was pretty good at it for the most part. I only allowed what I could have handled in my life. I didn't have a problem with saying "no" to things that I believed would dishonor God or would overwhelm me or complicate my peace. I prioritized what needed to be done first and I tackled the least important things when I was able to.

But when God told me to let Him have the instrument or control panel, I got a little uneasy in my flesh. I said to God "Lord, I am high up in this airplane, are you sure you know what you are doing?" Now of course we *know* God knows what he's doing at ALL times. However, my flesh had a hard time believing that especially when I felt I was in full control of the altitude I was flying through. The Word says, "that many are the plans in the mind of a man, but it is the purpose of the LORD that will stand." (*English Standard Version Bible*, Proverbs 19.21).

In my mind, I thought "Lord, it's easy to trust you when I haven't left earth. It is easy to trust you when I have concrete underneath my feet. However, high up in this airplane, where my flesh *really* needs to have full control, it's hard for me to relinquish the panel controls to you.

And in my mind, I heard "Trust the Lord" (*King James Version Bible*, Proverbs 3.5).

What I have noticed in the course of giving God full control is this: The first several flights I admittedly said "No God. I got this." During this time, I also admit that either I crashed the plane or I damaged the plane by not listening and trusting God. But little by little, I slowly handed over the control panels in my life and my faith and trust was strength in Him.

Metaphorically speaking, it is easy to trust God when we are on the ground and when we have stability and gravity under our feet. But it can be difficult to trust God when we are in midair and there's the uncertainty of the unknown; especially when we are facing a major decision.

I remember I was driving on the highway alone, cruising in my vehicle. The evening was changing to nightfall and it eventually turned to darkness quickly. In the far distance, I saw a car who had just put on its emergency lights and pulled over to the side of the road. I prayed and asked God if I should help. I try to err on the side of caution when it comes to helping someone at night especially when my own night vision is not 20/20. I kept asking God "ARE YOU SURE? ARE YOU SURE I will be safe?" Yes and amen flashed in my mind (KJV, 2 Corinthians 1.20). And because I **knew** God's voice, I pulled over. Now, my body was shaking in fear (although my spirit had peace) because I didn't know what to expect. I didn't know how many people were in the car when I pulled up? I didn't know if this was an ambush of some sort. But again, I recognized God's voice and obeyed. I got out of my car and cautiously walked to the driver's side door. A lady partially rolled down her window and I asked her if she needed assistance. She said no, she was fine and that help was on the way. I understood that God was testing me. He wanted to see if I would obey his voice, even in a situation that may have been scary for me (KJV, Psalms 26.2). My faith was strengthened from that test. And over time, it became easier and easier to know and to trust His voice. The key is **knowing** God's voice! The blessing is in the obeying part.

Let God be in authority over your control panels. Let Him be the controller of your plane. Let God be in control of your thoughts, your decisions, and the direction you take in life.

Let God guide your steps. He knows the way. Soar a little higher in Him. God can see what we cannot see. He knows your destiny. We have purpose in Christ. He's in control of all the modules in my life now. He steers my life, my journey, and my destination. When I allow God to be God in my life, things turn out better than expected. I reach His destination for my life. I reach His will for my life. I reach His purpose for my life.

Sometimes we only see what the radar on the control panel registers to us. Sometimes we only hear what the weatherman has told us. The weatherman sees the weather shifting and changing ahead of us. But God sees more.

Go higher! Take the limits off of God.

Sometimes in our attempt to achieve our goals, we may come up short because we are not reaching high enough. When God says in his Word His ways are higher than ours, we need to trust God, and allow Him to guide us to higher heights, believing that God can do the impossible (KJV, Isaiah 55.9). "Now to him who is able to do immeasurably more than all we ask or imagine, according to his power that is at work within us." (*New International Version Bible*, Ephesians 3.20).

One of the hardest things to do is to give up the control and allow God to steer us into our destiny. We sit in the cockpit with limited knowledge. We know how to take off on the runway with our limited knowledge. We know how to keep the plane at an altitude that is safe with our limited knowledge.

However, when God encourages us to come up a little higher spiritually, we panic and think "but what if something goes wrong? What if we crash because we went higher than the manual told us to?" When we have heard the voice of God succinctly, we can **trust** that we will not fail. Other people have failed because they **didn't** go higher in their business, in their education, in their ministry. They failed to extend themselves to see the manifestation of what God can do in and through them. They failed to see the mighty power of God by not reaching the top of the mountain.

- We fail because we stop trying. - "Trust in the LORD with all your heart and lean not on your own understanding" (NIV, Proverbs 3.5).
- We fail because we don't risk going higher in God. - "The king was overjoyed and gave orders to lift Daniel out of the den. When Daniel was lifted from the den, no wound was found on him, because he had trusted in his God" (NIV, Daniel 6.23).
- We fail because of fear. - "When I am afraid, I put my trust in you. In God, whose word I praise" (NIV, Psalms 56.3-4).

Give God the control panels over every area of your life.

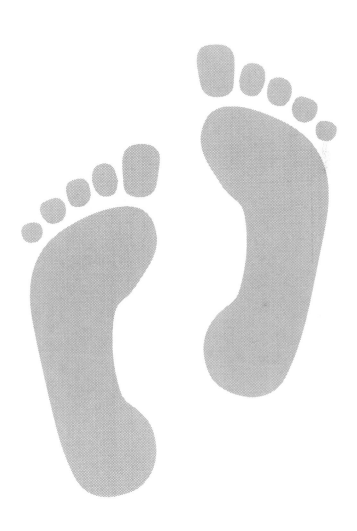

Chapter 2
IT STARTS AT HOME

No family is perfect. There is some kind of dysfunctionality going on in **every** household. Unfortunately, nobody is exempt. Hopefully your family is healthy enough to carry on some wonderful traditions. "Train up a child in the way he should go; even when he is old he will not depart from it" (ESV, Proverbs 22.6).

When you are reviewing your life's past decisions and direction in life, you may have thought "I could have done somethings better." But remember it's never too late to be a better family with the help of the Lord. We know there is no time capsule that can transport you backwards to relive, relearn, or rediscover a better way. You may not be able to change the past. What had already been done is done. But you can spare the future and make some corrections. You can still be responsible in changing those negative patterns, those generational woes that are destined to filter through to the next generation.

We are all born with influence. We influence someone. There is someone who admires and values us (whether it is positive or negative). We are born to affect someone in our lifetime and it usually starts at home, in our family nucleus. Our values generally come from childhood. Whether we are living in a 2-member household or a 20-member household, values are formed, cultivated, and enforced.

We learn these values (whether positive or negative), we adopt them and mesh them into our beliefs and behaviors. Values are learned through watching, hearing, and speaking.

God has always intended the family unit to be healthy, thriving and strong. Unfortunately, sometimes that does not happen because of the situation, circumstances, and sometimes sin that has filtered through to the next generation. Repeated negative patterns such as pornography, drug addictions, jealousy, and vanity have replaced sexual sacredness, independence, understanding, and self-effacement. "Do not be deceived: God is not mocked, for whatever one sows, that will he also reap. For the one who sows to his own flesh will from the flesh reap corruption, but the one who sows to the Spirit will from the Spirit reap eternal life" (ESV, Galatians 6.7-8).

I believe some of us are in a repeated cycle, making it harder for the next generation in our family to break patterns for a better healthier way of life.

God loves his family. You as a believer are a part of his family. He wants to help us with our nuclear family dynamics. He wants to help us heal. He wants to help us break chains of negativity. He wants to free us from our own mental prison. God wants us to be better for ourselves as an individual and for our family that is carrying our legacy.

Pray and ask God to help you to create healthier values for your family and for yourself. Ask God to help you break those cycles and negative patterns in your life.

It is time for change, it's time for a better future….it starts with US.

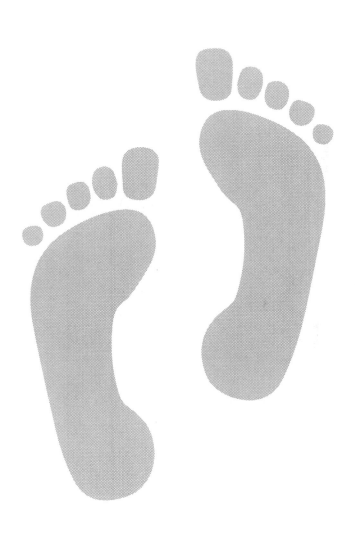

Chapter 3
REAL LOVE

Most of us want love. We want that connection with that special person. We want to feel protected and safe. We want all the trappings of a healthy love but we will settle for Pseudo love instead of reaching for what we deserve…REAL LOVE.

When we are desperately seeking love or hanging on to the pseudo love that we have, sometimes we only see the word love and not the negative word that may be in front of it like "toxic love, tainted love, bad love, wrong kind of love, good for nothing love, dangerous love, destructive love, poisonous or obsessive love."

We are so focused on the word love that we blind ourselves to the reality of the type of love we have. In our minds we convince ourselves that as long as it has the word love in it, it's good enough. We can't see that we have the wrong type of love when it's toxic. We reassure ourselves that this type of love is better than nothing. We tell ourselves "well, he has seen all my flaws and accepts me for who I am" or "no one else has given me this type of attention, I've got to hang on to it." But at what cost? At the expense of your self-esteem? At the expense of your self-worth? At the expense of your self-respect? At the cost of your goals and dreams? At the expense of true happiness? Or at the expense of the future God created for you?

One of the reasons I believe we settle is because we have settled for negative parts of ourselves. We have settled in our flaws. We have settled in our pain. We have settled in our proclivities. We have settled in what we don't deserve, and in return, we have **attracted** the same. We attract people who don't care about themselves, who don't love themselves or people who have a hard time giving love. We attract people who consider themselves worthless.

When we value ourselves, we love ourselves, and we appreciate ourselves. In return, we attract people with the same mindset, and that can equate to a HEALTHY type of love.

A healthy love that motivates you to grow closer to God. It encourages you to complete your goals with no selfish motives. A healthy love that knows how to love you through their relationship with God. Does a love like that exists?

Yes, healthy love does exist. Yes, real love is attainable. Yes, it's never too late for you to have the right kind of love.

Spending time in God's love builds your self-esteem and breaks downs those insecurities so that you can be healthy for the right kind of love. Allow God to show you your worth and your value. God can dissolve your flaws and your deficiencies to where you only see how amazing you are. God can fill you with His love that extend beyond human love so that you can attract the right kind of intimacy. "The one who gets wisdom loves life; the one who cherishes understanding will soon prosper." (NIV, Proverbs 19.8).

Quit being in a hurry to find a human to love. We are so used to needing a body to hug, a body to hold us, a body to cuddle up to, but when you allow love of God to consume you, it will **feel** like there *is* a body that is holding you and hugging you. "How priceless is your unfailing love, O God! People take refuge in the shadow of your wings" (NIV, Psalms 36.7).

Accept God's love. Allow God to change the way you see yourself and let Him prepare you for what seems to be rare nowadays... HEALTHY love, GOOD love, POSITIVE love, REAL love, God's love, and the RIGHT kind of love.

Chapter 4
DROWNING IN SIN

When we have allowed sin to consume us, we may feel some resistance when trying to find our way back to God. Oxford Dictionary describes sin as "an immoral act considered to be a transgression against divine law." When we yield to sin there is something supernatural that happens that is not obvious to the sinner. When we invite sin into our lives, sin then starts wrapping itself around us very subtly. The more we indulge into transgressions, the more it starts wrapping itself around our will power, and it becomes harder to let go and walk away. When the enemy has a hold on our spirit, he simply does not want us to leave his sinful pleasures. When we decide to walk away from our transgressions, the enemy use guilt and shame to keep us from returning to God.

God is there to pull us out of sin!

The problem is when we try to minimize the transgression, we initially think we can dabble in it and quickly escape from it when we convince ourselves we are in control. However, once we give into sin, it (meaning the sin) shakes hands with your spirit while wrapping its tentacles around your hand, thus make the grip much harder to release. Sin then injects fears, shame, insecurities, guilt, etc. into your spirit. Sin blocks our spiritual judgment and only gives us the temporary pleasure of the flesh. Once that transgression has a hold on us, it slowly starts depleting your spirit without you realizing it.

Picture this: You are on a beach and sin is calling you into the water. Now you know the height of the water begins shallow and gradually gets deeper into the bottomless ocean. You know you are a good swimmer, so you semi analyze the distance. You decide to play around in the shallow of sin. You feel confident you can easily get out in the shallow area when you are ready, but then you start testing the waters little by little, edging more and more further into the deep of the ocean. At this point you have convinced yourself you are in full control and you are going to enjoy sin a little bit more. The water is warm and the waves are brushing up on your body just right. It is feeling good to your flesh. Then, as we stay in the water of sin, we are being carried out by the waves further and further from the beach. Further away from where we started. Sin is a powerful spirit and can pull us further into the deep.

God does not want you to drown in your transgressions. He has his arms open wide, ready to pull you up from the sharks that want to see you die in sin. "For the wages of sin is death, but the free gift of God is eternal life in Christ Jesus our Lord" (NIV, Romans 6.23).

Therefore, if you are drowning, return to Christ in true repentance, and God will save your life (again). He will teach you how to say "no" to the enemy if you trust God. You see there is no struggle when you say "no" to sin. Why, because sin cannot touch you when you say no. There is no spiritual handshake involved. But when you agree to experiment with sin, to indulge in sin, in *any amount*, there is a spiritual handshake in agreement that happens with you and the enemy. That spiritual agreement with the enemy entraps your spirit and causes you to stumble in your walk with the Lord. "No temptation has overtaken you that is not common to man. God is faithful, and he will not let you be tempted beyond your ability, but with the temptation he will also provide the way of escape, that you may be able to endure it" (NIV, 1 Corinthians 10.13).

Remember: Whether you are stuck in an addiction or whether you are in spiritual, mental, or physical bondage, call on the name of the Lord for the saving of your soul!

"This know also, that in the last days perilous times shall come. For men shall be lovers of their own selves, covetous, boasters, proud, blasphemers, disobedient to parents, unthankful, unholy, Without natural affection, trucebreakers, false accusers, incontinent, fierce, despisers of those that are good, Traitors, heady, high-minded, lovers of pleasures more than lovers of God; Having a form of godliness, but denying the power thereof: from such turn away" (KJV, 2 Timothy 3.1-5).

"Now the works of the flesh are evident: sexual immorality, impurity, sensuality, idolatry, sorcery, enmity, strife, jealousy, fits of anger, rivalries, dissensions, divisions, envy, drunkenness, orgies, and things like these. I warn you, as I warned you before, that those who do such things will not inherit the kingdom of God" (NIV, Galatians 5.19-21).

God can free you from that handshake mistake! As long as you have breath in your body, it is not too late to turn from the errors you made!

Chapter 5
GOD IS PLEASED WITH YOU

God is pleased with you when you make attempts to serve Him (KJV, Hebrew 6.10).

God is pleased with you when you love one another through Him (KJV, 1 Peter 4.8).

God is pleased with you when you try to obey Him (KJV, John 14.15).

God is pleased with you when you read the Word of God to get closer to Him (KJV, Psalms 1.1-2).

God is pleased when you worship Him (KJV, Ephesian 5.19).

God is pleased with you when you have faith in Him (KJV, Hebrew 11.6).

God is pleased with you when you pray to connect to Him (KJV, Matthew 6.9-13).

God is pleased with you when you stay in His Will (KJV, John 15.1-27).

God is pleased with you when you trust His direction (KJV, Psalms 9.10).

God is pleased with you when you love God with all your heart (KJV, 1 John 4.19).

God is pleased with you when you encourage someone, even with a simple smile (KJV, Galatians 6.1).

God is pleased with you when you help one another (KJV, Luke 6.38).

God is pleased with you when you are considerate (KJV, Romans 3.23).

God is pleased with you when you are nonjudgmental of others (KJV, Luke 6.37).

God is pleased with you when you care for others (KJV, Galatians 6.10).

God is pleased with you when you pray or intercede for others (KJV, 1Timothy 2.1).

Allow God and His angels to cheer you on…as you *keep* pleasing Him!

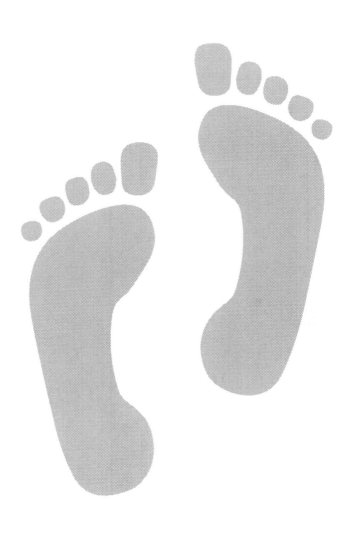

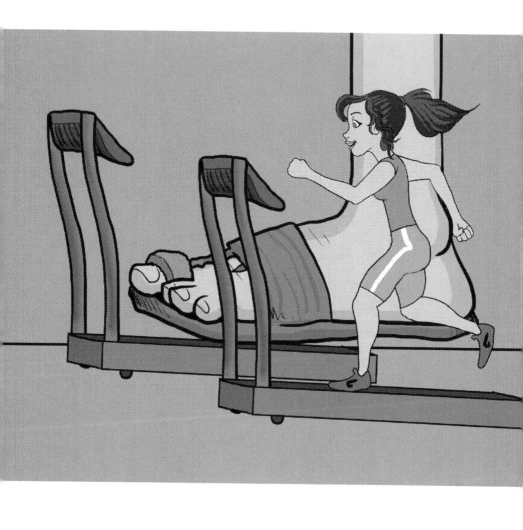

Chapter 6
EXERCISE YOUR FAITH MUSCLES

What are faith muscles?

Faith muscles are tools that you would use to strengthen your beliefs. Faith muscles are muscles you build through answered prayers (past and present) for instance. It is remembering how God brought you out of a difficult time in your life or provided a way for you through circumstances that did not seem favorable for you. It is seeing the hand of God over your life and in your situations. You can find stories in the bible that can strengthen your faith but it is better when you can see the hand of God working in *your* own life, because it becomes *your* real-life story and *your* testament of the goodness of God.

When you pray as a believer, you are tapping into the One who created the universe; The Creator himself. The One who allowed His Son to die for our sins. The One who has His DNA stamped on all of us. He has given *you* an unique code that only you carry. When you pray you are connecting to our Lord Jesus Christ with your special code that God recognizes through your own way of communicating with Him. You are the one who can touch the hem of His garment through your code. Remember the story of Blind Bartimaeus? He was a beggar and heard Jesus strolling through town. He was desperate to be healed and cried out to Jesus but His entourage intervened and told him to be silent. Bartimaeus continued shouting with his unique code. He hollered from his heart and Jesus heard him and healed him (KJV, Mark 10.46-52). You may think you do not know how to pray or how to reach heaven, but keep praying with your heart (your code). God hears you!

How does faith muscles develop?

It is like holding weights in your hands for a lengthy duration of time. Your muscles would eventually get tired, but they also develop strength each time you hold those weights in your hands. When we believe God can answer our prayers and we stand on His promises, we are holding the weights in ours hands. We are holding onto the promises. Every time we let go pre-maturely the evidence of our results is not vivid in our biceps. We get frustrated because we do not see God moving rapidly enough in our lives. We MUST *hold* on to the weights with patience and faith believing, to see the results we desire from The Lord. Doing this *builds* faith muscles.

Did you know there are other ways to build faith muscles?

You can build spiritual muscles through sacrificing by fasting unto the Lord (which is a type of religious sacrament), educating yourself in the Word of God, worshipping in songs and hymns, or witnessing to others with your faith in Jesus Christ.

Fasting:

Fasting is a religious sacrament that crucifies the flesh. Fasting builds spiritual muscles by denying the flesh when you do it unto The Lord. You push away food, drinks, T.V. shows, or anything that is a craving or an addiction to draw yourself and your spirit closer to God. It is denying your flesh the cravings it desires. You are saying "Lord you mean more to me than what my flesh craves." It is a way of yielding and disciplining yourself to Christ. There are various ways of fasting. Pastor Jentezen Franklin is a best-seller author of many books, including the book called "Fasting." It is an insightful book and can help you understand on a much deeper level the different types of fasting. "While they were worshiping the LORD and fasting, the Holy Spirit said, "Set apart for me Barnabas and Saul for the work to which I have called them" (NIV, Acts 13:2).

Worship:

Worship is singing psalms and make melody unto The Lord. It is like a special father/daughter dance but in song. Worship takes you to a place that is open, free, peaceful, and clear in the spirit. It is that euphoric feeling you get while worshiping the Almighty God.

Some people have a favorite place to visit, i.e. Bahamas, Florida, or Las Vegas. God has a favorite place for you that leads you into the spiritual realm through worship. You fill the atmosphere around you with angels through worship. His presence consumes you and your faith muscles are strengthened. "...then was a widow until she was eighty-four. She never left the temple but worshiped night and day, fasting and praying" (NIV, Luke 2.37).

The Word of God:

The Word of God builds faith muscles by pouring into you like a health drink. You may struggle with comprehending some passages in the bible but whatever you digest is still healthy to your body. When you open the Word of God and attempt to read it with an open heart (a willing heart), Christ deposits spiritual nuggets into your spirit without you realizing it. If you find yourself struggling to understand God's Word, first pray with expectancy and desire, then read. The more you read, the more God will reveal His Word to your spirit. He will give you the revelation through your consistency. "For the word of God is alive and active. Sharper than any double-edged sword, it penetrates even to dividing soul and spirit, joints and marrow; it judges the thoughts and attitudes of the heart" (NIV, Hebrew 4.12).

Witnessing:

Build spiritual muscles through witnessing is an effective way of increasing your strength. You are exercising the faith in God through your testimony. You are putting into action what God has taught you over the years. Witnessing utilizes the impartation of God's wisdom. When you share the gospel, you teach others how to be strong through their trials and that builds your muscles as you build theirs. God pours into you so you can pour into others. You wear the armor of God when you share the Word of God. "Let your light so shine before men, that they may see your good works, and glorify your Father which is in heaven" (KJV, Matthew 5.16)

So, let us start building and flexing our spiritual muscles!

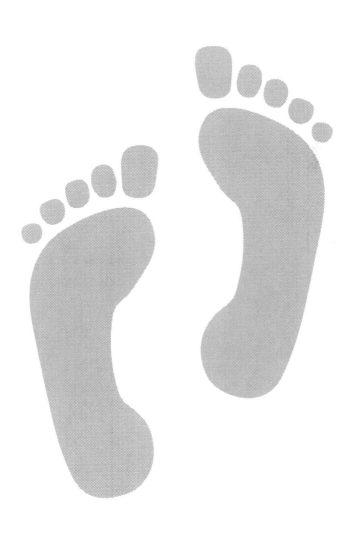

Chapter 7
ADVENTURE INTO THE WORD

What I admire about the Word of God is the fact that there are so many various perspectives and angles to glean from in every story in the bible. The Bible (Word of God) is a fascinating book! For instance, if you were asked to put a title to the story of Jacob, Leah and Rachel in the bible while exploring all the reasons that match the title, you could come up with numerous topics such as:

Leah, The Woman Who Wasn't Loved
Leah Was Highly Favored And Blessed
Jacob, A Man Torn Between Two Women
Jealousy In The Camp
Jacob Reaping What He Sow

The Things A Man Would Do For The Woman He Loves…and the list goes on.

God's Word is alive and well and fits every trial, tribulation and victory we could ever face. Once we understand God on the basic level, we need to take a stroll or adventure in His Word and discover more of Him.

There are endless paths to explore, no wrong paths. It is like going into a big city, downtown. When you get there, you see a pleather of shops, eateries, and places to explore. Every shop is different from the other but it is all in the same place, downtown. Each store offers something different but it is all in the same place, downtown.

Each shop's layout, content, decorating ideas have dissimilarities from the next shop but it is all in the same area, downtown. Each stop or restaurant has a different chronical (history) but they are all connected to the same location, downtown.

The stories in the Word of God operate the same way as the metaphor I was using. You could focus on the clothing or shoes in your studies. You could focus on the miracles and the fact that God did not perform the same miracle twice. You could focus on the various kinds of worship, various ways God helped the leaders win the battles, or you could make it specific to your need and what you are going through. There are so many avenues to explore!

Spend time on the path and explore the many facets of Christ. Each adventure is like taking a trip to a foreign country and immersing into the cultural there. The Bible is amazing! God's book never gets stagnated when you seek His knowledge.

The Word of God says:

"Your word is a lamp to my feet and a light to my path" (ESV, Psalms 119.105).

"All Scripture is breathed out by God and profitable for teaching, for reproof, for correction, and for training in righteousness" (ESV, 2 Timothy 3.16).

Take your next adventure with Christ and allow Him to take you through His beautiful history so you build strength for *your* today.

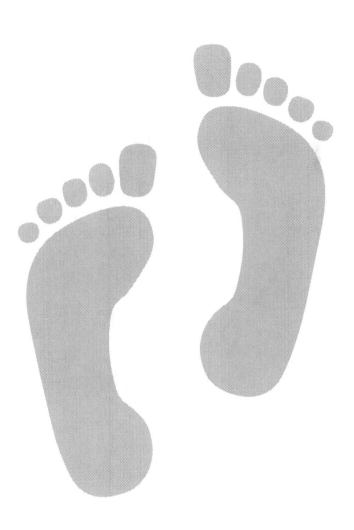

Chapter 8
DR JESUS

Hurt, pain, and past trauma can make quite an impact on your life and the course of it. Nobody I know likes to experience pain or have PTSD (post-traumatic stress disorder) from past trauma in their lives.

I am reminded of my father when he blurred the boundary lines in my relationship with him. His eyes morally blinded and tainted what was supposed to have been a healthy daughter and father bond which negativity impacted my life. I eventually did not know how to show affection towards my dad without him twisting it into something sexual. In return, it caused me to be less affectionate to my kids for fear that they would see it as something else other than the mother and child relationship that God ordained. Since I was not taught the correct way to love, I had difficulties loving my own children. I instead developed other appropriate ways to show my affection until God delivered me from my trauma. God had to heal me. I received the healing and deliverance from the damage my natural father inflicted on me. Glory!! "He healeth the broken in heart, and bindeth up their wounds" (NIV, Psalms 147.3). "The righteous cry, and the LORD heareth, and delivereth them out of all their troubles. The LORD is nigh unto them that are of a broken heart; and saveth such as be of a contrite spirit. Many are the afflictions of the righteous: but the LORD delivereth him out of them all. He keepeth all his bones: not one of them is broken" (NIV, Psalms 34.17-20).

When Jesus died on the cross it was not just for our sins, but for our hurts, our pain, and our PTSD too. The beatings that Jesus suffered, the name callings, the spiting, the neglect, the demoralization, and being ostracized was also for those who experienced that at well. Jesus went through worse pain and suffering than what we could ever experience. I believe Jesus made sure He covered everything we could ever go through so that we could experience healing. Without Christ there would be no way for us to abolish our hurts.

Receiving healing or deliverance frees you to move forward into a better and healthy future. Your past will no longer impact your present and it will change your future with a much stronger and wiser progress.

Did you know that God can transform your lemons in life into a beautiful bouquet of fresh lemon scented flower? What? There is no such thing as a lemon becoming a scented flower, you say. Remember God can do the miraculous. "Grace be with all them that love our LORD Jesus Christ in sincerity" (KJV, Ephesians 6.24). God can have you smelling fresh scent lemons from any flower to prove that He is God!

I remember I was living in an apartment years ago and was praying to God about the good parts I was missing in my dad. I had tears welling in my eyes in remembering the good things he taught me over the years. My dad loved sunflowers and I told God that the following year I would plant sunflowers in the front of my apartment in remembrance of my dad. There was nothing planted in the front for most of the eleven years I had lived there, but God saw fit to plant sunflowers that same year. Less than two months later, sunflowers miraculously appeared, growing in the front of my apartment. I never told anyone my conversation with God. I was shocked and amazed through my joyful tears and I remember God simply telling me "you can have those sunflowers now." He saw fit to grow them shortly after my talk with God about my dad. I *know* for myself that God can do the imaginable. Watch God turn your trauma into beautiful fresh lemon scented flowers!

Your pain for his peace. Your hurt for his complete healing. Your trauma for His PTSD (peace, trust, strength, and direction).

Chapter 9
GOD'S COVERING

What is God's covering? I believe it is an inherited covering when you initially accept salvation, although I am only speaking of one way in particular. The minute you give your life to Christ, you receive this invisible, spiritual covering from God. It is like a protection barrier that sets you a part from the world. It opens the door for God to speak to you. It opens the door for God to minister to you soul. It comes with guardian angels that protect you and warrior angels that fight for you in the spirit. It comes with the ability to tape into the spiritual realm. It is a great feeling. It is a covering knowing that God can do what man cannot do in the flesh. "He will cover you with his feathers, and under his wings you will find refuge; his faithfulness will be your shield and rampart" (NIV, Psalms 91.4).

I believe once God gives you that covering, you have to stay under it by staying connected to Him in prayer, His Word, and any other way that keeps you locked in the arms of God, which is like an umbrella. Once you are covered, it becomes your job to stay under that coverage through trusting God. When God moves left in our lives and we move left with God, we stay under that covering. When God moves right and we decide we are moving left, we are moving away from his covering. For instance, if God told you to wait before permanently leaving a job you were getting irritated with, and you left anyway, you would have moved away from the covering of God and His provisions for you. Maybe God wanted you to bless someone there, or maybe He was trying to work more patience in you; but because you put in your two weeks' notice earlier than God's expected date, you may have delayed a blessing that you needed. Here is another example: If God told you that the person you were dating was not compatible enough for you and you heed to God's warning/advice by walking away, you are staying in His Will, his covering. If you ignore the warning and continue in the unhealthy relationship, then you would have moved *away* from God's Will and away from his covering.

Not only your lack of trust in God can draw you away from God's covering, but your lack of devotion and prayer life can also draw you away from the covering God placed over you. Remember *you* are responsible for staying under the covering. God provides the covering but it is *our* job to work hard to stay under that umbrella.

Imagine seeing some people with umbrellas on a raining day and some people without an umbrella. When you do not have the umbrella (covering) over you, you run the risk of catching a cold, the flu or getting your new hairstyle or outfit drenched. I believe it works very similar in the spirit. You are more vulnerable to the enemy's spiritual attacks when you are not under the umbrella of God.

Now do not misunderstand me, you may get hit with a few sprinkles of raindrops (a few trials and tests) from time to time while being *under* the umbrella covering, but you are mostly dry and protected otherwise. The more we stay connected to our Heavenly Father, the more we are protected. The more we obey God's Word, the stronger the umbrella covering is.

Why do I need a covering? Because there are things that only God can do for you that human flesh cannot. The world cannot give you supernatural peace in the mist of chaos but God can. The world cannot hide you from enemy's attacks but God can. I remember on my job there was someone that was trying to get me fired unbeknownst to me. I had no idea because he was always in my face smiling, seemingly being nice. But behind my back, God revealed to me that he had sinister motives. So, I prayed over my job and rebuked any attacks over me, my job, and my life. God prevailed!

The world cannot give you promotions like God can. The world looks at your resume and says you are not qualified. But God looks at the skills He has given to you and qualifies you for the job when we trust His provisions, under the covering.

Having a covering is like having a mini entourage of angels that go with you wherever you go. It is kind of like added protection when you have a relationship with God.

In the bible, David was a faithful servant to Saul, King of Israel for a number of years. King Saul valued David and rewarded him with blessings as the years went on. King Saul ended up having animosity and bitterness for David and eventually he made attempts to kill him twice before God told David to run to the hills for safety. David hid in the cave for years until the coast was cleared. Because of David's deep relationship with the Lord, David had advance warning on the enemy's tricks. God made provisions to keep David safe from King Saul's threats (KJV, 1 Samuel 18-27). David was under the umbrella.

Remember Leah in the bible, the woman who was a worshipper but was unloved by her husband? Her husband Jacob loved Rachel, his other wife, more. Leah had a deep relationship with the Lord and God favored her even though she was not loved by her own husband. She ended up having more boys than Rachel, which was a symbol of prosperity in biblical times. Leah birthed half of the tribe of Israel; six boys and one girl! Wow! God covered her and blessed her through her tears. Leah was under the umbrella (KJV, Genesis 29).

God *still* operates in similar ways today. Receiving salvation and His covering are only the beginning of some amazing things God does for his children.

What are the benefits of having a covering? Promotions, blessings, increases, insight, supernatural wisdom, guidance, and favor, just to name a few.

It is daily blessings from sun up to sun down.

"The LORD will guard your going out and your coming in from this time forth and forever" (NIV, Psalms 121.8).

There is guidance and direction for your life.

"Trust in the LORD with all your heart, and do not lean on your own understanding. In all your ways acknowledge him, and he will make straight your paths" (NIV, Proverbs 3.5-6).

"I will instruct you and teach you in the way you should go; I will counsel you with my eye upon you" (NIV, Psalms 32.8).

There is insight in understanding people and how to handle someone specifically. "Beloved, never avenge yourselves, but leave it to the wrath of God, for it is written, "Vengeance is mine, I will repay, says the Lord" (NIV, Romans 12.19).

There is supernatural wisdom in learning how to prosper in life.

"I do not cease to give thanks for you, remembering you in my prayers, that the God of our Lord Jesus Christ, the Father of glory, may give you a spirit of wisdom and of revelation in the knowledge of him, having the eyes of your hearts enlightened, that you may know what is the hope to which he has called you, what are the riches of his glorious inheritance in the saints, and what is the immeasurable greatness of his power toward us who believe, according to the working of his great might" (NIV, Ephesians 1.16–19).

There is unmerited favor with others including your enemy.

"When a man's ways please the LORD, he maketh even his enemies to be at peace with him" (KJV, Proverbs 16.7).

God's covering is essential in this day and time. We never know what is going to happen from day to day. But, at least under God's provision, we can rest in peace knowing our Almighty God is in control and we are walking in His Will.

So, make sure you are under the umbrella of God.

Chapter 10
WAITING TAKES TIME

Waiting is a word society does not seem to want to utilize anymore. It is a skill that needs to be exercised to see its' benefits. With all the latest gadgets and technologies that allows us to rapidly accomplished things, we do not have a need to "wait" anymore. If we now have been granted the option to **"not"** wait, then…why wait?

Humm….

We know that you can be in a situation where waiting is **not** beneficial. For instance, if someone is abusing you mentally or physically, God may have you to exit that relationship as fast or as early as possible.

But waiting can be the best option in other situations.

God says "But many that are first shall be last; and the last shall be first" (NIV, Matthew 19.30). Society seems to have adopted the "instant gratification" mindset. We rush to get things done fast, quick, and in a hurry. Because society has thrived in that, it has a difficult time *waiting* for results. We went from mixing the cookie ingredients for the oven to just eating cookie dough! And the phrase "Patience is virtue" seems to have gotten lost in the shuffle of commercials that emphasizes "quick and easy!"

However, if waiting is not mandatory, why wait? Is it wasted time to wait? If time seemed to present itself, why wait? If I wait for it, would it be worth the wait? There is no guarantee that it will be there later, so why not have it right now?

Waiting gives your physical and mental mind something it need that being impatient cannot:

Waiting helps you to make less mistakes. You get to see the entire picture when you wait. You can examine all sides of a situation, when you take the time to ponder. This increases your confidence and builds faith. For instance, when a salesman tries to pressure you to buy something on the spot for a deal. Sometimes it is wise to review the information and take a few days to see if it fits into your lifestyle. It gives you time to make a wise decision and not a hasty one. It gives you time to go over the pros and cons of the product.

Waiting develops perseverance. It builds staying power in your ability to wait. It builds "peace" in situations when you wait on God's timing. You are stronger when you opt out of rushing into a decision. You become steadfast and unmovable (KJV, 1 Corinthians 15.58).

Waiting helps to understand tolerance. You become calm under pressure. When you see other people get irate about petty things (small, unimportant matters), you can see the level in which you will not allow yourself to get to. Your tolerance becomes a blessing in various situations. By exercising patience and developing a certain amount of allowance, you can become a blessing to others when they are stressed. You become the calming person that helps others through with a little humor or a pleasant conversation to loosen or relax others around you during a difficult time of waiting.

Waiting helps you to enjoy it more. Good things come to those who wait. There is a sense of appreciation for what you waited for. A certain kind of satisfaction in knowing that you waited for it.

For instance, when you are building a business. It takes time. And when you wait for the growth with every step you take, you slowly start seeing it. It then builds and grows into a huge business. You do not mess around with pansy schemes or schemes that bribe the American people of their hard-working money. You build slow and methodically until it grows. I believe God blesses things when they are honest and built with His grace.

So, let patience have its virtue in your life!

Chapter 11
FRUITS OF THE SPIRIT

It is about healthy eating. It is about a natural healthy diet straight from God. "But the fruit of the Spirit is love, joy, peace, forbearance, kindness, goodness, faithfulness, gentleness and self-control. Against such things there is no law. Those who belong to Christ Jesus have crucified the flesh with its passions and desires. Since we live by the Spirit, let us keep in step with the Spirit. Let us not become conceited, provoking and envying each other" (NIV, Galatians 5.22-23).

Let's look at why it is so important to digest into your soul the fruits of the Spirit:

Love- Love is the first one on the list. It is the staple of foods. This is the most important fruit of all. This fruit should be eaten every day and with all meals including snacks. Love is the core root of everything God stands for. He loves us by allowing His only begotten Son to die for us so that we have a hope in salvation. God is perfect love. In his salvation, he teaches us how to love through his spirit.

Let all that you do be done in love. The bible tells us that "Love is patient, love is kind. It does not envy, it does not boast, it is not proud. It does not dishonor others, it is not self-seeking, it is not easily angered, it keeps no record of wrongs. Love does not delight in evil but rejoices with the truth. It always protects, always trusts, always hopes, always perseveres. Love never fails. But where there are prophecies, they will cease; where there are tongues, they will be stilled; where there is knowledge, it will pass away" (NIV, 1 Corinthians 13.4-8).

Joy- The second on the list. "The Joy of the Lord is our strength" (KJV, Nehemiah 8.10)! Being joyful and sad simultaneously cannot happen when it is God's joy that you are displaying. Christ gives you that joy that can stomp out depression, sadness, and despair. God's joy comes with a supernatural strength that is built into it. It is different from happiness. Happiness is when you create it and it only lasts as long as the event that made you happy. Joy comes from God and it can last a lifetime when you continue to operate in it. It is capable of lifting up other people's spirits around you because of the built-in strength it holds.

Peace-This fruit is sometimes hard to achieve. People multitask and try to accomplish 101 things in the day. We juggle family, spouses, children, jobs, chores, agendas, etc. The peace I am referring to is the peace that surpasses all understanding (KJV, Philippians 4.7). It is the reassurance that we are in His Will. It is the spiritual peace that gives us the confidence to move forward or the confidence to take a stand in something. This type of fruit only comes from God because he can settle a conflicting matter in your spirit. When you are making a decision about a situation, pray about it, and ask for God confirmation to do or not to do, through his peace.

Forbearance (patience)- It is the fruit that says "good things come to those who wait." When we allow this fruit to ripen before we eat it, it becomes one of the sweetest fruit in the fruits of the spirit. This fruit requires you to trust God for His timing. We may want that promotion, a spouse, or material things we have been eye-balling for a while, but when we go to God in prayer about our desires, we must exercise the fruit of patience. God's timing is not our timing, which may frustrate some of us but when we trust that He wants the best for us, we then keep our flesh in subjection to God's Will through patience. The flesh wants to do things on its own because it feels like God is not working fast enough in our current situation. However, waiting on God will not only strengthen your spirit but the rewards are far more than you can imagine (KJV, Philippians 4.6).

Kindness-This fruit goes a long way. Even just a tiny bite (like a smile) can do wonders for someone. We are living in a world that is hurting. A world that is depressed and oppressed. We are living in a place where one kind act can change the life of someone's spirit. Your smile says "I care." Saying the words "God loves you!" can fill a broken heart. Showing an act of kindness to someone is saying "you matter." God knows the importance of making someone feel loved through kindness, so remember you can do a lot with this fruit. It goes a long way in healing someone (KJV, Romans 15.2).

Goodness (righteous)- You will recognize them by their fruits (KJV, Matthew 7.20). This fruit evolves through the four seasons. It is not tossed to and from. It takes an uncompromising stance. It upholds integrity and standards. This fruit you eat is constantly getting its nutrients from the Lord on a regular basis. This fruit has put God first and flesh on the back burner. People know who you represent by your actions. The fruit of this spirit bears witness to who you serve. Although you may try to fool people in the flesh, your fruit will *always* reveal if you are serving God or mammon, so eat this fruit with all your heart and soul unto the Lord.

Faithfulness- The loyalty fruit. The fruit that brings out the regularity in serving God. It represents walking with the Lord consistently. It represents doing what is right whether anyone sees you or not. It is staying faithful behind closed doors when no one is looking at your Christian walk. It is still doing the right thing when no one is present. This fruit is dedicated to serving God in season and out of season (KJV, Hebrew 10.23).

Gentleness-The delicate fruit. The fruit that seasons your words with salt. This fruit reminds you to extend grace to others. Sometimes we as believers can be judgmental in our assessments of people, but when we eat the "gentleness" fruit, we are sympathizing with others through the eyes of God (KJV, Colossians 4.6).

Self-Control- The fruit that controls temptations. This fruit can self-regulate your behavior and emotions so that you are mentally balanced. It helps to control your thoughts so that you are not dwelling on negative or unhealthy beliefs. It controls those impulses to keep you healthy physically. This fruit helps you to overcome the lust of eyes, lust of the flesh, and the pride of life.

So, as the saying goes "an apple a day, keeps the doctor away." When we digest and operate in the fruits of the spirit on a regular basis, we are keeping our spiritual bodies healthy not only for ourselves but for others around us. Let us feast daily on God's fruits!

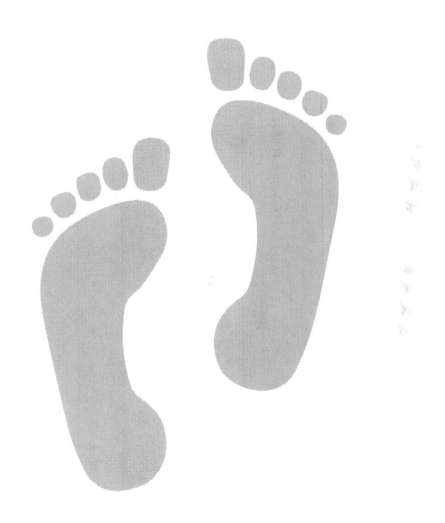

Chapter 12
SINGLENESS CAN BE A DANGEROUS THING

Ahhhh, it can be relaxing travelling on a motorcycle, wind in your hair, just you and the open road. Serenity is comforting at times. It gives you a chance to unwind, clear your mind, and meditate by yourself. It is a chance to regroup and destress if needed. However, sometimes being alone in our walk with God is not beneficial to the soul.

Some people may say "I don't need church. I can watch church on T.V." Or "What do I need church for, I *am* the church?" I believe we take things out of context to suit our personal exigencies when it is really the enemy's needs we are accommodating. Because of the hurt that we may have experienced at a church, or any offenses that traumatized us from a past church event, we can feel the need to isolate ourselves from other church members and even from church itself. The enemy wants us to be at home and alone. The enemy does not want us to be in a church setting where there is strength in numbers. The enemy does not want us to be wiser than he is. The enemy uses our offenses and the hurts to trap us and to keep us from healing and growing. The bible says "not giving up meeting together, as some are in the habit of doing, but encouraging one another—and all the more as you see the Day approaching" (NIV, Hebrews 10.25).

Singleness can be a dangerous thing when you decide to go solo spiritually.

Think about a pack of wolves that preyed on an animal, separated from the pack. They always look for the weakest link. When you are spiritually alone, you are subject to the enemy's attack, frequently. Your frustrations and hurt feelings can keep you from persevering. We need to search the heart of God to see if we have legitimate reasons that would prevent us from attending church. If so, then in our prayer time, we need to pray for guidance to a place that is right and safe for you. If you are unable to attend a church for health reasons (for example), God understands that. If your offenses are *not* validated by God, then I believe it is time to deal with those petty offenses and stay near the pack.

God uses people to refine you. You grow in God *with* people of the same faith.
God uses people to buffer us, to test us, and to challenge us.
God uses people to show his love through us.
God uses people to teach us how to love and care for others.
God uses people to teach us how to get along with others for His name sake.
God uses people to strengthen prayers.

Remember there is strength in unity. Do you remember the Battle of Jericho in Joshua Chapter 6? The Israelites were trying to conqueror their land in Canaan as God had promised them. They marched around the walls of Jericho once a day for six days and then on the seventh day they marched around the wall seven times. Upon doing this, the walls came crashing down showing that there is strength in unity.

Isolation is the enemy's strategy. The adversary feeds you excuses to keep you from the pack. He plays on your insecurities and pride to keep you from growing in grace. You as a believer are vital to the *body* of Christ. God wants you to stay connected to keep your spirit strong. You learn how to grow through others. You get wisdom and understanding from others saints.

Remember there is strength in numbers.

Chapter 13
KEEP MOVING YOUR FEET

Your feet are made for carrying your weight. Your feet are designed to take you places. They are created to move you into the direction you were meant to go. Your feet are made for you to take action either by walking or running towards that task.

Don't allow your feet to stand still, immoveable. Move them forward. Take steps towards the goals you want to achieve in life. If you have a desire to sing in the choir, go and sign up! If you are wanting to join the altar committee, take the initiative to make that happen, even if you were physically born with no feet, you still have spiritual feet that will guide you into what you are capable of doing. In Christ, the sky is the limit. "I can do all things through him who gives me strength" (NIV, Philippians 4.13).

Sometimes we can sit too long admiring how far we have come in our journey with God. We can get complacent and think we have arrived. We prop our feet up. We get that much needed pedicure and decide we have done enough for God, and stop. Keep moving!

Now exhaustion or burn-out can play a role in you contemplating if you should take a permanent vacation from ministry, or you may have gotten a little overwhelmed in serving, and a short break may be necessary to rejuvenate your spirit. I believe serving God is for life, no matter how great or small you serve. There is no retirement in Christ. As long as you have breath in your body, there is always something to do for God.

Why is that, you may ask? The devil does not stop trying to attack God's people in some way or another. God needs all eyes on deck, serving Him at any capacity to thwart the enemy's plan over our loved ones, friends, and neighbors as much as we can, wherever we can. Remember the enemy comes only to "steal, kill and destroy" (NIV, John 10.10).

God may start you off doing great things and then later in life slow you down for whatever reason such as age, health, etc. He may start you off serving in little things as He increases you into bigger things that will bring Him glory. Either way, keep moving in Him. Do not stop. God may call you to take a break but you should never completely stop.

If you were used to travelling and can no longer travel for ministry, then there is something locally you can do. If you were used to overseeing a large group of people but now your group has dispersed, then there is something else for you to do. Do not get stagnated in your Christ-walk. Pick up a book, learn something more about God and educate someone about your discovery. God wants us to keep learning, keep discovering, keep serving, and keep moving forward in Him.

Whether it is doing a wellness check on someone, sending out an encouraging card to strengthen someone, or creating a needed ministry, keep your feet moving. "Whatever your hand finds to do, do *it* with your might; for *there is* no work or device or knowledge or wisdom in the grave where you are going" (*New King James Version Bible*, Ecclesiastic 9.10).

Whether your feet are moving fast or they have to move slow in serving God, just keep moving!

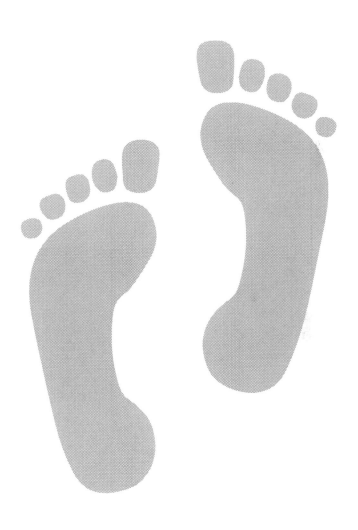

Chapter 14
GOD'S GPS SYSTEM

God has a plan and a direction for our lives. "I know the plans I have for you" declares the Lord, "plans to prosper you and not to harm you, plans to give you hope and a future" (NIV, Jeremiah 29.11). God has the correct GPS (Global Positioning System) navigation system coordinates for our lives to get us to where he has ordained for us to be. Your destination could be exercising your talent globally, starting a business/ program that gives back to others, ministry that connects you to the world, or a gift that you were born with that God want to use to bless someone else with.

Consequently, what happens is we sometimes get off course in the process of getting there. God's GPS tells us to travel right and we purposely travel left because we decided that travelling left was better for us. We looked down the left side of the road with our natural eyes and made a decision out of fear or ego to go off course. So, what happens then?

In God's grace and mercy, He re-calculates the GPS for us that will still lead to His purpose. Here is the thing to remember: His plan for your life may have some hills and valleys that you need to go through to get to your destiny but it is *still* the *safest* way. It is the *protected* way God has chosen for your life to get you there with minimal influence from the enemy. When we decide to go the opposite of God's plan, we have opened the door to much more than we bargained for. There is much more danger on the path that we chose for ourselves. It is like we are entering our own path at our own risk. That is not a chance you should take. When you see signs that tells you "Danger Ahead or Enter At Your Own Risk" in areas that are prohibited, in the spirit realm it works the same way. We do not know what is on the other side of that sign but because of our rebellious or stubborn nature, we sometimes take that chance only to find out it was not what we thought it was. The road was either much harder, maybe too many predators we ran into and barely escaped with our lives, or what we thought was a wellspring of water was only empty promises from the enemy that has left us dehydrated and broken. Keep in mind, God is looking down from His throne.

God can **see** the easiest path for you. And since you are on ground level, you can only see as far as your eyes will allow you to see and it is limited. So, TRUST God for the plans that he has for YOU. The life that God has created for you is a beautiful, rewarding life. Trust God. "Now faith is confidence in what we hope for and assurance about what we do not see" (NIV, Hebrews 11.1).

Stay the course and get to your future with divine protection.

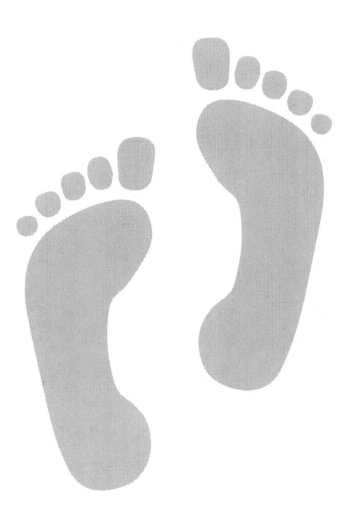

Chapter 15
PROMOTION COMES FROM GOD

On the job is where we implement the principles we have learned in church, in Sunday school, in bible study, or at home in devotions. It is taking the text book of spiritual learning and applying them to real life situations. At work is one of the places that our salvation is examined. It is a breeding ground for testing and teaching us how to love difficult people. It helps us to work with those who do not have the same faith. It helps us to understand the importance of attendance, how to work in a team setting, etc. It is the experience we need and the training ground that is necessary for our spiritual growth when we have applied the Word of God to our situations on the job. You cannot read the Word or attend bible classes and assume you know how to love your brethren without being tested in that area.

On the streets or at home, it is easy to avoid those that have a negative spirit. You simply do not have to invite them to your house or you can simply ignore them by staying home. On the job, you are required to work alongside people for the betterment of the company. You are required to show team skills as most employers want you have this kind of attribute. You **need** the experience. Allow God to teach you how to develop traits you may lack (love, patience, cooperation, trusting, giving) on the job. God uses people to strengthen us. He uses people to mature us to the character He wants us to exemplify in our spiritual walk.

Did you know that promotion comes from God? "The LORD makes poor and rich; He brings low, He also exalts" (NIV, 1 Samuel 2.7).

We may think promotion comes from the employer (man) but when we know enough about God, we see that God is the one that promotes His people. Have you ever prayed for another job and got it without having to apply? Have you ever been promoted when you did not expect it? God is the one that is behind the scenes making things happen for you. I used to get upset when I saw others being promoted before me especially when I felt like I was in line for that promotion, but God revealed me that he was not ready for me to be elevated yet into that position. I admit I was feeling some kind of way but I had to allow God to work on my pride. In due time, I eventually got promoted. Sometimes we can feel as if we may be losing opportunities if man decides who gets promoted and who doesn't. It can feel like man is in control of our next level. I know, I used to feel this way. When I learned who God was in my life, I learned that He is the one who promotes His people. He is the one who puts it in the heart of man to promote you and I. "For everyone who exalts himself will be humbled, and he who humbles himself will be exalted" (NIV, Luke 14.11).

You may have a stubborn boss who simply does not like you because of your faith, and may refuse to give you the promotion you earnestly deserve. When you pray and seek God, He will open that door in our lives in due time. Several things can happen: Either God will move things around on that job, that will cause you to be promoted despite having a stubborn boss, or God will create another job, better promotion, more money, or better opportunities somewhere else. God does the supernatural things that cannot be controlled by man when we trust Him. We dare not to limit God. We dare not to keep God in a container when we know and believe He is bigger than our situation. We only need to think outside the box and give God time to breathe his own way of promoting us, into our spirits. Our focus is just to trust God and his timing and not limit our advancements to the current job alone. "Therefore humble yourselves under the mighty hand of God, that He may exalt you at the proper time" (NIV, 1 Peter 5.6).

Promotion comes in different forms. You can do well on your job, but get a promotion in your ministry. Or someone could reward you with a gift on the job for your efforts in production. That is still a promotion. Take the limits off God and allow God to reward/promote you with what He has for you at that time. "Then the king promoted Daniel and gave him many great gifts; and he made him ruler over the whole province of Babylon, and chief administrator over all the wise *men* of Babylon" (NKJV, Daniel 2.48-49). Daniel petitioned the king and he set Shadrach, Meshach, and Abednego over the affairs of the province of Babylon; but Daniel *sat* in the gate of the king.

We never want to get ahead of God. He sees what we do not see. We may think we need that promotion right now because of our circumstances or financial obligations but maybe God sees in the moment there is something that could render us more problems that we did not see, even when we think we knows the ins and outs of a situation. Remember we are limited in our knowledge; God sees and knows much more than we do. He sees the bigger picture.

In the meantime, do well on the job. Every day put forth your best effort. Strive to get along with your co-workers and bosses. Ask God to teach you how to wait patiently for God to elevate you into another position. He will cause someone to see your efforts. He will put it on someone's heart to give you that increase. As you work and do it wholeheartedly unto the Lord, God will show someone your efforts. God sees your hard work and He will encourage someone else to see the same thing.

Chapter 16
GOD'S MESSAGE IS PERSONAL

It is personal! God's message is personal!

I have always found a fascination in the message given by the pastor.

For instance, let us say I had Bible study over the week with myself and nobody but me knew what I reviewed, researched, or learned except God. The following Sunday, I hear the pastor mention in his sermon a scripture I had reviewed in that past week or he mentions something I was studying in his message. When this happens, I get excited and dumbfounded all in the same emotion! How did this happen? How did the pastor know what I was studying? I believe God's message was personal. I believe it was an encouragement to let me know that God was connecting His spirit with my spirit in His Word. Whether God purposely drew me into reading a certain passage of the Bible or God simply made a sporadic connection with me to keep me growing, I simply think it is amazing how God does that.

I often wondered if God had others members of the church read the same thing over the week so that we all can connect to the pastor's sermon. Or if other church members were studying something different during the week but God mysteriously allowed the pastor to mention *their* scriptures or topic to the individual's ears. "Now to him who is able to do immeasurably more than all we ask or imagine, according to his power that is at work within us, to him be glory in the church and in Christ Jesus throughout all generations, for ever and ever! Amen" (NIV, Ephesians 3.20-21).

Let us say you were at your favorite musical concert, in a crowd packed with people. Now the musician does not know you or acknowledge you as he is performing on stage. You were hidden out of sight amongst the crowd. All of a sudden, you hear the musician call your name. You are first startled but then when he mentions your full name, you know he is **clearly** talking to you, and you think "Wow, in a crowd full of strangers he acknowledges ME. I matter." That is how I felt when God mentions something I was studying in the pastor's message, as if the preacher had **me** and only **me** in mind when he decided on his message. I believe God does that with many of us. His message is personal and he connects our spirit to His spirit in a personal way. I matter to God. You matter to God. God is concerned about our growth in Him.

So, let us continue to connect with God as He connects to us personally.

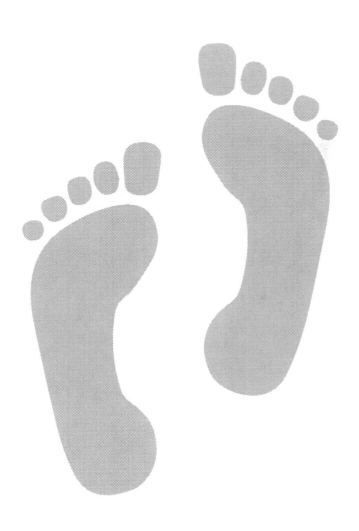

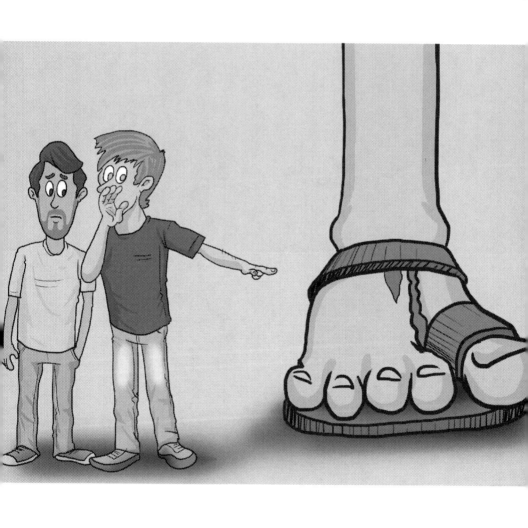

Chapter 17
SHHHH, DON'T GOSSIP

Did you know little over half of the people who participated in a survey I was researching enjoyed hearing gossip? It is virtually promoted everywhere; in our commercials, Netflix movies, companies we work for, schools, home, and amongst our family and friends. We cannot escape it.

As defined in the Oxford Dictionary, Gossip means "casual or unconstrained conversation or reports about other people, typically involving details that are not confirmed as being true."

I personally think it is interesting some people would rather believe the gossip than the truth. I think I know why.

When it comes to truth, truth is generally plain; bland. It is just facts. I believe the truth can sometimes resembles the dullest gray on the color scheme. Truth is usually not exciting to the hearer of gossip. It usually does not come with extras or emotions that tickle the hearer.

On the other hand, gossip, I believe, is the bells and whistles. It is a built-in "hype man." You get the extra vernacular, the extra adjectives, and colorful words that "hype" up the story, fabricating it.

Gossip is more exciting and more appealing to the ears. It is entertaining with extra feelings and emotions. It may be enjoyable to hear, but the ramifications are not worth it if you are operating in the love of God.

Gossip in any form can simply destroy someone's life. It can leave deep scars on the heart and soul, cause bankruptcy (financially and mentally), and can cause someone to lose valuable relationships (as well as business).

It is a backbiting and wicked thing to do to others. God even hates gossip. "There are six things that the Lord hates, seven that are an abomination to him: haughty eyes, a lying tongue, and hands that shed innocent blood, a heart that devises wicked plans, feet that make haste to run to evil, a false witness who breathes out lies, and one who sows discord among brothers. We do not understand the power of the tongue"(ESV, Proverbs 6.16-19). "Death and life are in the power of the tongue..."(KJV, Proverbs 18.21-23).

We all have perceptions. Our perception is infused into our DNA. We are going to have a different outlook on life. My sister and I grew up in the same house, saw the same things, but our perspectives were different. She saw herself being a big sister to me. I saw her as being bossy, and that annoyed me growing up. We were born and wired as two individual people with two different lenses on life.

Because we all come with different perspectives, we are going to see things differently. One person may see forgiveness, and another may see chastisement. One may see leniency—another judgment.

We are not all wired the same way. Our way of thinking is different from someone else. We must keep that in mind.

Remember the internet craze with the blue dress and the gray dress. The world was divided on the color of the dresses. Let us see what the Word of God says before we speak.

"Finally, brethren, whatsoever things are true, whatsoever things are honest, whatsoever things are just, whatsoever things are pure, whatsoever things are lovely, whatsoever things are of good report; if there be any virtue, and if there be any praise, think on these things" (KJV, Philippians 4.8). This should be our cognitive process before exercising our mouth.

Our personalities are not designed for everyone's acceptance, and sometimes the offenses of others are not really offenses.

Sometimes the offenses are petty issues. People's pettiness can be dramatized and blown up to make the offense worse than what it was and at the same time cause others to stay clear of the person they are gossiping about. The tongue can be a horrible weapon.

If you ever find yourself in someone's confabulation (gossip), Before you do anything, you may need to first calm yourself from getting agitated about the situation, then go into spiritual warfare and ask God what to do. Every situation is different, according to God's purpose and plan. He may tell you to confront the person. He may tell you to wait for his signal, or God may tell you that if you trust Him, He will get the justice you need. God's strategy is the *best* because he sees the ins and outs and more of what you cannot see.

I remember I was lied on several times. The first time I was so angry, I wanted to find another church. When it happened again less than a year later, I was fuming. I went to God. I had to deal with my anger and insecurities first, so I prayed. He gave me peace and in my mind I saw Jeremiah 51:36, "I will defend you." And God was right! Glory!

I believe we have the power to control our tongue. We must control our words. We must refrain from listening to gossip and send a "no tolerance" message to the gossiper. "The tongue also is a fire, a world of evil among the parts of the body. It corrupts the whole body, sets the whole course of one's life on fire, and is itself set on fire by hell.

All kinds of animals, birds, reptiles, and sea creatures are being tamed and have been tamed by mankind, but no human being can tame the tongue. It is a restless evil, full of deadly poison" (NIV, James 3.6-8).

Therefore, Child of God, let us speak words of healing and not words of destruction.

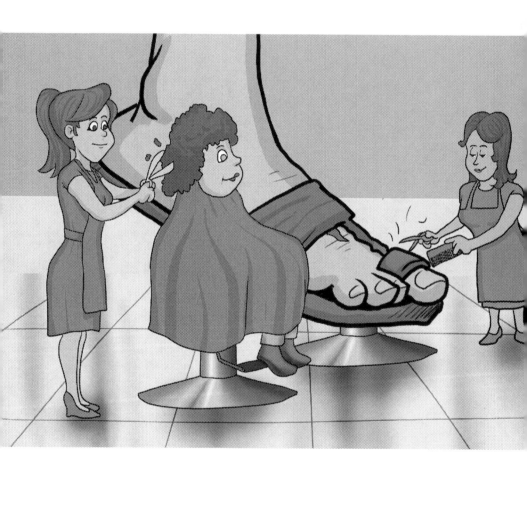

Chapter 18
LOVING YOURSELF

Sometimes we get so caught up in maintaining our surroundings. We may have meetings to attend, a family to take care of, job duties, school obligations, and personal responsibilities that need to be balanced. In the process of learning how to juggle all of the demands on our plate, we can neglect loving and caring for ourselves. "Come unto me, all [ye] that labor and are heavy laden, and I will give you rest" (KJV, Matthew 11.28).

We put so much emphasis on each obligation on our plate that we forget about giving ourselves some attention. We should not forget to take care of ourselves; things like getting our hair done, buying a new outfit or suit, buying our favorite lunch, sitting in a quiet park to eat it while relaxing in the cool breeze. It could be giving yourself a home facial before reading your favorite book from time to time. Another idea could be going to the gym, taking that hike, or walking along the beach for exercise while you meditate on the peace in God. You are saying to yourself, "I am alive, I love me, and I matter."

I remember early in my walk with the Lord I was so busy doing things for God, my family, and my job that I neglected myself. I was caught up in others' wellbeing that I forgot to give myself some "me" time.

I put myself on the backburner on the list of priorities. At one point, I felt like I was walking around in a body without an identity. It troubled me so much that I spoke to a close friend about my concerns. They helped me bring balance back to my life. Eventually, I learned how to love myself again in the midst of my duties, obligations, responsibilities, etc.

I learned that for me to continue caring for others, I had to care for ME. Allow God to help you "love you" as you balance everything else around you.

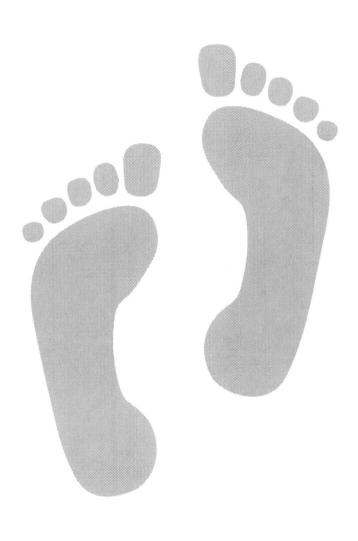

Chapter 19
VACATIONING WITH GOD

Are you going on vacation or a "stay-cation"? Take God with you.

Are you going to a fun-filled event (or outing)? Take God with you.

Are you going to a family function? Include God in your plans.

We can sometimes add God in our day-to-day routine, but sometimes exclude Him when we do something out of the norm, like taking a vacation.

What do I mean by that?

We do not plan that God may use us to bless someone while we are on vacation. We forget to consider that just because we are taking a trip does not mean that God is taking a break from needing us. Being a servant of God is a permanent thing. "Preach the word; be instant in season, out of season; reprove, rebuke, exhort with all longsuffering and doctrine" (KJV, 2 Timothy 4.2). God needs to be in everything that we do. If God puts that urgency in your spirit to do something, we should be prepared to oblige the Holy Spirit if it is His Will, even on vacation.

A few years ago, my spiritual mom and her close friend were blessed to go to Israel. During this trip, neither one expected to be used by God. They made plans to explore pertinent location spots and the local eateries that offered tasty entrees. They planned to pick up a few souvenirs and relax in the shade during most of their trip, but God had something else that He included, in mind. My spiritual mom ended up witnessing to a gentleman that needed encouraging words of God. She never expected that God would need her on vacation, but He did, and she was ready!

We never know what God is doing. Depending on your situation, He may not need your services at all during your vacation. God may feel that you have over-exhausted yourself in your daily life. He may want you to take time out to replenish yourself in The Holy Spirit. Sometimes rest is good for the soul.

We believers are angels doing the work of the Lord. You may have to fix someone's tire, give a monetary donation, or pass out a gospel tract. You might have to witness to someone or provide food. We never know what God has planned for us, but we should always stay in preparation, ready at any given moment.

We should always thank God for the vacation, but simultaneously, we should be prayerful and ready to respond to His calling. We need to meditate in our spirits, "Lord, I am going to enjoy this vacation to the fullest, but if you need me, I'm here!"

Remember, as God blesses others through you, and He continues to reinvest in your spirit, it is an automatic exchange.

You reap what you sow. Sow into others, reap the rewards back.

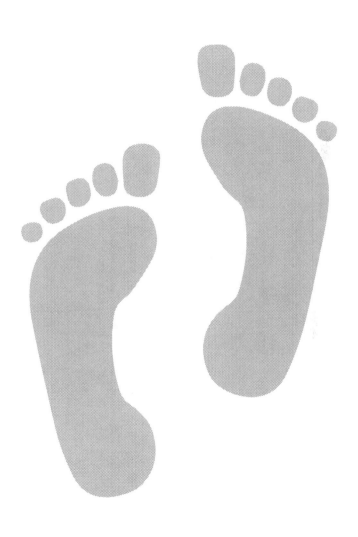

Chapter 20
LEARN FROM YOUR LESSONS

Our lives come with teachable moments; as we learn different lessons along the way, the lessons cultivate and shape our destiny.

Lessons teach us what mistakes should not be repeated.
Lessons guide us to the truth.
Lessons remind us to be wise and to exercise wisdom.
Lessons can shape our disposition to create in us a better person.
Lessons are great teachers. They educate us on the do's to get the preference we desire and the don'ts to avoid the unfavorable results.
Lessons can show us what failure looks like.

Jesus taught his disciples so many lessons on discipleship. Jesus used their biases, their character flaws to make them better. "Then the eleven disciples went away into Galilee, into a mountain where Jesus had appointed them. And when they saw him, they worshipped him: but some doubted. And Jesus came and spake unto them, saying, All power is given unto me in heaven and the earth. Go ye therefore, and teach all nations, baptizing them in the name of the Father, and of the Son, and of the Holy Ghost: Teaching them to observe all things whatsoever I have commanded you: and, lo, I am with you always, even unto the end of the world. Amen" (KJV, Matthew 28.16-20). I believe God wants to make you better through your experiences and trials.

Lessons are a part of life even though we are not fond of the lesson at times. Life will test us regularly. Unexpectant trials will surface and positive and negative things will come from those trials. Whether we see the glass as half-full by focusing on the positives or half-empty by focusing on the negative is up to you.

It is always best to learn from others as *much* as possible. Humble yourself and let other people's trials and mistakes be your teacher as often as possible. "A wise man will hear and increase in learning, and a man of understanding will acquire wise counsel" (NIV, Proverbs 1.5). One day you will be a teacher for someone else, knowingly and unknowingly.

Let your lessons be your path to perfection (spiritual maturity) (KJV, Matthew 5.48).

Let your lessons lead you into a worthy life that is pleasing to God (KJV, Colossian 1.10).

Let your lessons protect you from repeating mistakes that keep you from growing in Christ (KJV, Proverbs 2.11).

Let your lessons shield you from becoming vulnerable again to the temptation of the enemy (KJV, 1 Corinthians 10.13).

Let your lessons strengthen you into a stronger child of God (KJV, 2 Thessalonians 3.3).

Let your lessons pave the way to righteous and holy living in Christ (KJV, 2 Samuel 22.3–4).

Learn from your fallacies. Learn from your mistakes through the Strength, Grace, and Mercy of God, and allow His love to sustain you through it (KJV, Psalms 121).

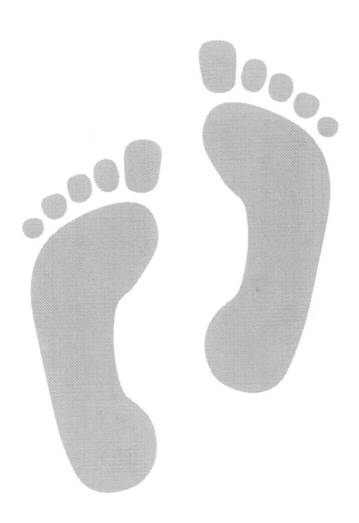

Chapter 21
LITTLE EXTRA LOVE

It is amazing to me to see how God's domestic animals have assisted humans throughout time. "The LORD is good to all; he has compassion on all he has made" (NIV, Psalms 145.9).

I have seen on social media various examples of animals protecting humans from endangerment. I saw on social media a cat protecting an unsuspecting toddler from a loose dog that was attempting to attack. I have seen animals defending the owner's home from wild predators or strangers. Animals that have that capability to protect and serve us are phenomenal. Animals are heroes.

Animals that have the disposition to nurture, care, and protect humans are like angels to us. Animals adapt to our lifestyle. I believe God uses what he created to help us in unsuspected ways. It may be a stray animal that defends us "out of the blue" when we need it or an animal that can give us a much-needed hug. God created animals to serve us as we serve them. "...O LORD, thou preservest man and beast" (KJV, Psalms 36.6).

I am reminded that there are so many reasons animals exist:

- To teach us how to love and care for something
- To love those who are lonely
- To assist us as working animals
- To guard and protect us (if necessary)

- To warn us if trouble is near (seeing-eye dogs, seizures detecting dogs, etc.)
- To love and comfort us through trauma, abuse, fear, hurt, etc.
- To mourn the loss of us when it is our turn to pass away
- To give us a sense of purpose in life

Animals are the "Little Extra Love" because of the extra that comes with animals. You get a little something extra when you love animals with their unique intelligent personalities, their eccentricity, and playful spirits. Through your love, you will see their wonderful disposition come to life.

So, do not abuse animals. They need you as much as you need them!

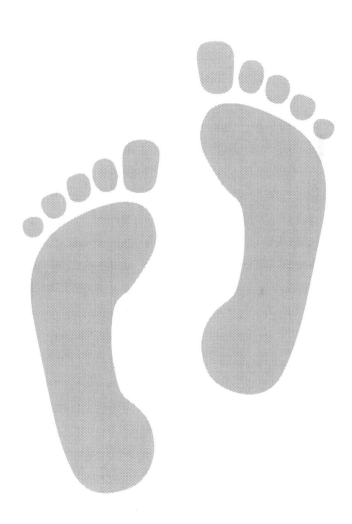

Chapter 22
"SELFIE"- PERCEPTION

When we take a selfie and post it on social media, we sometimes get so caught up in other people's opinions about us.

Why?

Because we value their opinions, and we appreciate the source of where it's coming from. In some instances, it can be a good thing if the opinion is positive, uplifting, and encouraging and helping you make a good impression for a job interview. You may have butterflies in your stomach about the interview, and need some positive words.

The problem lies when we allow negative opinions to affect our lives immensely. Those negative opinions can push us into a depressed state, or we could end up feeling suicidal.

Picture this: you are ecstatic because you won $1,000,000 (tax-free). Someone takes a picture of you (with your permission) holding the money, and you are smiling from ear to ear, thrilled to be the proud owner of a lot of money. Unbeknownst to you, that picture got shared around on social media, and some people have made some negative comments about it. They either didn't like what you were wearing, or they didn't like the fact that it was you that won all that money.

In the **picture** you didn't hear what they were saying about you because you were in the **picture**. A picture cannot hear. Your excited facial expression in the **picture** did not change upon hearing the negative comments because it was a **picture**. You were still happy and oblivious to what was being said about you. You still expressed happiness and cheerfulness as you were focused on your winnings, in the **picture**.

That is what self-worth looks like, you are not affected by people's comments. You are not being bothered by people who disagree with who you are. It is by knowing who you are, respecting yourself, and valuing yourself regardless of who does not value or respect you. When you do not conform to the world's opinions, you can say, "who cares what they think!" Do not conform to the pattern of this world, but be transformed by the renewing of your mind. "Then you will be able to test and approve what God's will is his good, pleasing and perfect will" (NIV, Roman 12.2).

When you *are* valuing the world's opinions more than God's opinion about you, then...

It's time for a "Selfie" examination.

It's time to "Selfie" analysis.

It's time to raise the bar on your "Selfie" esteem.

Self-esteem is sometimes based on external factors, whether you have the desired income or have that desired weight loss. Today you may have the confidence to beat your sibling in a game of checkers, but tomorrow, if you played against a master in checkers, you may feel defeated before the game even started.

Raising the bar on our self-esteem means building up our self-awareness. It means getting to a place where no matter what comes or goes, no matter the circumstances, our self-worth stays the same, in the positive zone. It means not allowing other people's opinions to dictate who you are as an individual.

How do you do that? You allow your inner self to attach itself to the inner part of God through earnest prayer and seeking to understand God and His love for you. "The effectual fervent prayer of a righteous man availeth much" (NIV, James 5.16).

Having self-acceptance frees us from the chains people place on us. It frees us from the mental bondage of people because of how they want to see us

Sometimes we get so focused on admiring others that we miss all the beautiful and unique attributes about ourselves. In the Word of God, the LORD said to Samuel, "Do not consider his appearance or his height, for I have rejected him. The LORD does not look at the things people look at things. People look at the outward appearance, but the LORD looks at the heart" (NIV,1 Samuel 16:7).

God is the one who created you and designed you with all your flaws, biases, deficiencies, disabilities, and yet you are *still* beautiful! It is *never* about what you see; it's *always* about what God sees.

They say beauty is in the eye of the beholder, but God that gave the beholder the eyes to see His beauty. The world is so caught up in its own "selfie" or image of what attractiveness is, but God is caught up in **your** beauty. You catch His eyes every time you breathe. God is caught up in how He made you, "fearfully and wonderfully made: marvelous are thy works" (KJV, Psalms 139.14).

Every time you dress in the mirror, every time you fix your hair, every time you take a selfie, say, "Lord, you look good on me," and then walk away with God's confidence!

Chapter 23
FIGHT UNTIL YOU SURRENDER

I am not talking about the physical aspect of fighting, but the mental part of the battle. You have to win the war in your mind first so that your actions can manifest your victory. Fighting with God until you surrender your will is ok. Just like Jacob in the bible, when he had some trepidations (fears) in his life (KJV, Genesis 32.22). He was worried about getting mutilated by his brother Esau over the birthright he stole. Jacob wrestled with a manifestation of God for a blessing of protection from his brother Esau. He fought God until God blessed him. He fought God until he was broken which ended up being his hip.

Have you ever struggled, giving God control in areas of your life? Let's say, for instance that God wanted you to write with your opposite hand for the rest of your life. You know how to write with the hand you normally use but to write a mere sentence with the opposite hand may be difficult for most of us. It requires more control and concentration. It probably requires moving at a slower pace, right?

You start off accepting God's desires for you. Shortly into it, you get frustrated because it takes too much time to get the letters right as you write with your opposite hand. You may get angry with God. You may say, "what's the point? This isn't making sense, God!" You may even go back to your regular writing style with the hand you usually write with. However, if you keep trying to write with the opposite hand in obedience, you will eventually get better at it. Then it will become the new normal for you.

When God advises us to do something, we sometimes buck against it. We sometimes rationalize why it does not make sense to us, or feel since we've been doing something a certain way, and it's a part of our character, then why change now?

That is the same way when we struggle with changing something in our lives that God believes we need to change. It may be a character flaw that you have been living with for years, but when we grow in God, it sometimes means that we need to be pruned again. Another layer needs to come off. When we accept God, we accept his salvation for us.

Sometimes he delivers us from many things at the beginning of our walk with Him, and sometimes, he takes his time and waits for the right time to prune us again. In the first season of our spiritual walk, it may have been an anger issue we developed over the years or a chronic need to please people too much that needed purging. In the next season of our spiritual walk, it might be something in our character that God feels is potentially harmful moving into our next season. Remember, we are always growing, learning, and perfecting (maturing) in Christ.

When you fight with God and surrender your all, it means *your will* is broken. You have completely capitulated (or surrendered) to God.

Here are some benefits when we wrestle with God:

Wrestling Keeps You. You are saying, "I want to be kept."

Jacob's hip was dislocated, but he would not let go of God until he blessed him. He was resolute (determined) in getting what he wanted. Wrestling keeps you in a place where you can hear God. You mesh with God in that wrestling match. You are close to His Word; you are close to His voice (KJV, Genesis 32.25).

If you have kids or have been around kids, it is a blessing when that child heeds to your warnings or advice the first time. It makes life as a parent or as a guardian easy, stress-free. On the other hand, when you have that one child that bucks like a bull over everything you say, you can quickly get irritated and think, "why does he have to be so hard-headed?"

We, as adults, are no different. We may obey God in like ten areas in our lives but fail to do the one thing (the 11th thing) that God has singled out as the most important one for us to overcome before we reach our next level. Remember, God is trying to perfect us (mature us) every day. Every day we yield to Him, we grow in perfection, and we grow more in His Will for us.

Working at a senior housing facility for many years has awarded me the opportunity to see this unfold. Residents there had attitudes that humored me on a regular basis. They would tattle on each other, fuss over frivolous things, and still had stubborn tendencies even when I was trying to keep them safe. I told my residents to keep their apartment doors locked because of people roaming up and down the hallways at night when the offices are closed. Half the time, my residents did not listen.

God sees us the same way; sometimes, we are stubborn, yet he still loves us. He loves that defiance in us. He wants us to wrangle or argue with Him. He created you; God formed you that way. Let

Him wrestle that resistance out of you." So, fight with Him until you surrender! Remember God's powerful and mighty. He can handle *us*.

You become stronger. I believe bull-headed or stubborn people make good warriors. We are God's formidable warriors, the ones He can put on the battlefield to win a war. We are made to rise above our infirmities. We were made for battle. That is why some of us wrestle. God wants to wrestle with your defiant strength. He knows you will relinquish your will if you keep fighting.

"He trains my hands for war and my fingers for battle" (NIV, Psalms 144.1).

"...though He was a Son, yet He learned obedience by the things which He suffered" (NKJV, Hebrews 5.8).

I heard a quote that said, "I know the way, but I learned it the hard way."

Most of us love God, but some of us have a hard time with obedience. If someone quoted "If you love me, keep my commands" (KJV, John 14.15), some of us may get offended and say, "I may not do everything God tells me, but I do love God, don't tell me I don't love God!"

But in your new level, God wants you to love him in a different capacity, one that requires more sacrifice in showing your love to Him. Growth spurts sometimes hurt, but grow anyway.

What exactly does a fight with God look like? It's fighting on your knees. It's standing or walking around your home, denouncing the enemy and giving God the victory. It's yelling at God if you need to (alone). It's de-stressing all your concerns, cares, and trepidations (fears) on Him in your prayer closet. You are taking it to the mat and fighting until you surrender! It's not letting go of God until he delivers you from yourself!

There were many Sundays I came to church exhausted because I knew I had been wrestling with God all week. In the spirit, I think I came in with a black eye and a busted tooth, but I kept at it until *my* will was finally broken. God wants you to do the same thing. It may be a tedious process, but keep at it.

Wrestling helps you to learn God's way and His Will for your life!

Wrestling keeps you wrapped in clutches of his arms!

Wrestling keeps you still, confined to one spot!

Wrestling also keeps you "in control," so you don't get "out of control."

So, fight or wrestle with God if you have to, until YOU surrender!

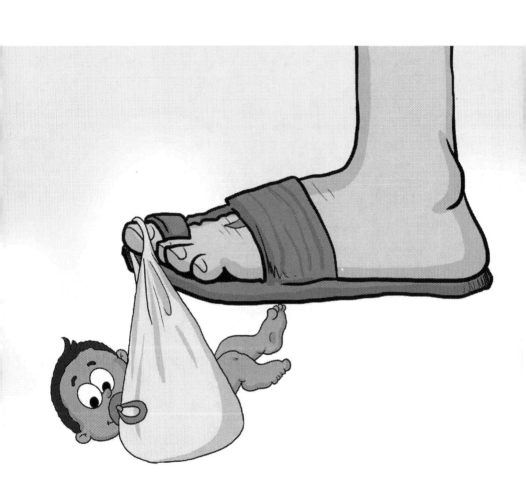

Chapter 24
YOU ARE CHOSEN

"I know the plans I have for you," says the Lord. You are born with a purpose. You are not an accident or an "oops" baby, no matter what someone may have told you. God chose you to be here. God did not make a mistake when he allowed you to be born. "For I know the plans I have for you," declares the LORD, "plans to prosper you and not to harm you, plans to give you hope and a future" (NIV, Jeremiah 29.11).

God wants to remind you:

Your purpose is greater than your situation, circumstances, and your need to just survive.

Your purpose is greater than your abuse or trauma.

Your purpose is greater than you.

You are created to make a fingerprint in this world.

Your unique DNA has an impact that influences the world.

Something as simple as a smile, thoughtfulness, or kind gesture from YOU can change the atmosphere around you.

You were born because God wants you to rise above your statistics.

God chose you to win; to succeed; to overcome.

God chose you through His mercy and grace to rise.

God chose you to confound the world.

God chose you to beat the odds.

God chose you to believe in Him that you can do anything.

God chose you to share the love of God through His love for you.

"For God so loved the world that he gave his one and only Son, that whoever believes in him shall not perish but have eternal life" (NIV, John 3.16).

For God did not send his Son into the world to condemn the world, but to save the world through him.

Whoever believes in him is not condemned, but whoever does not believe stands condemned already because they have not believed in the name of God's one and only Son.

God loves you THAT much!

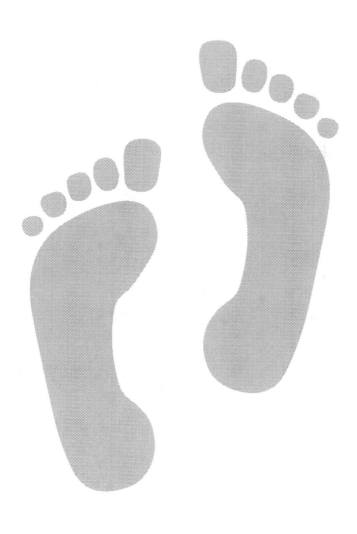

Chapter 25
TAME YOUR EMOTIONS

One minute, you are high on a roller coaster of emotions. The next minute, you are in the valley in your feelings, vacillating in your spirit on what to do in the situation you are in.

American Christian Pastor, speaker, and author Dr. Tony Evans once said, "Your emotions don't have intellect." In other words, your emotions do not have common sense. It is like a three-year-old child who wants candy for their breakfast, lunch, and dinner. A three-year-old child does not understand why they can't have the candy for all three meals of the day. Their emotions just want what it wants without logic. When that child gains intellect and learns the importance of eating healthy meals with an occasional snack, their common sense will dominate their emotions.

It is time to get off that emotional roller coaster. It is time to get your emotions under subjection! God wants you to allow His spirit to rule your emotions. "By myself, I can do nothing; I judge only as I hear, and my judgment is just, for I seek not to please myself but him who sent me" (NIV, John 5.30).

God's spirit tames those "out of control" emotions of the flesh.

God's spirit knows how to keep your emotions within the boundaries of His will.

When you are in your emotions, it feels real. It is real, but sometimes our emotions can overwhelm us and cause us to lose control of our decision-making or thought processing skills. For example, say you are at the local grocery store. You happen to see your favorite celebrity shopping for produce. You want to get their autograph before they disappear. If the thought of walking up to them and asking them politely for their autograph appeals to you, then you have successfully kept your emotions in check.

If the thought of you screaming with excitement and pushing people out of the way as you run full speed to get that autograph appeals to your more, then I would say you need some work on taming your emotions.

When you are "in your feelings," your emotions are controlling how you feel. Remember, since your emotions don't have intellect, **you** are the one that can control the temperature of your emotions. You are the one that decides how much emotions you are willing to express. When we go through a breakup in a relationship, it can hurt. Sometimes we can get into a deep depression over it that ends up negatively affecting our lives, or maybe we didn't get what we wanted. We allow our emotions to spiral out of control.

Learn to control your emotions. God wants us to be balanced in all that we do. You have the power to feel differently than what your emotions are accustomed to. We can sometimes become addicted to the roller coaster ride so much that it looks "normal" to us and we fail to recognize how imbalanced our emotions have been in our lives.

We can be around someone for so long that we pick up their addiction and not be aware of it. Sometimes it can also be a chemical imbalance or learned behavior through our defense mechanisms.

Habits can be changed. The bible says "put off your old self, which belongs to your former manner of life and is corrupt through deceitful desires, and to be renewed in the spirit of your minds, and to put on the new self, created after the likeness of God in true righteousness and holiness" (ESV, Ephesians 4.22-24).

Ask God to help you to change those habits. Free yourself from that wild emotional ride by asking God what is His strategy for you, so you can adopt a new healthy way of expressing emotions. Even through the tough times as well as the good times.

Practice makes perfect!

Chapter 26
LEVEL UP IN GOD

"Level up" means progressing to the next level. Every year, we have a birthday. It signifies another year older, even if we don't celebrate it with friends or family. Every year, you acquire more wisdom and knowledge than the previous year. With every passing year, you gain more experience than the year before.

When a child reaches the age to drive a vehicle or to work in the restaurant business, they have "leveled up" in life. They have progressed forward in life. When a person is able to retire from their long-term employment, they have "leveled up" in life. They now get to reap the fruit of their labor with their retirement benefits. I believe it works the same way in the body of Christ. We as believers "level up" in our spiritual growth.

Maturity in Christ comes with overcoming trials and tribulations. Someone may have trouble with practicing patience, for instance, but if they keep emulating and following God's personal strategy for them, then as they overcome, they will be "leveling up" in their spiritual walk with the Lord! One minute the impatient driver may be yelling at the other driver on the road ahead, and the next minute, he or she is rejoicing about not feeling compelled to yell anymore because God delivered them from it! That's a "level up" that person has reached in their journey with Christ. That's graduating! I believe God's graduation system is very similar to the graduation system in school. What do I mean?

In school, you are given 13 years (that includes kindergarten for most states) to graduate with an H.S. Diploma. Every year, during each grade level, you have to meet a certain level of academic scores before you can graduate to the next grade level.

In Christ, we all have flaws, and God stated in His Word that no man is perfect. "For all have sinned, and come short of the glory of God" (KJV, Romans 3.23). So, Mr. Spoon (imaginary name I picked for this scenario) for instance, may have trouble with pride, anxiety issues, and or may be too blunt when they communicate. And Ms. Fork on the other hand, may have some jealousy and abusive issues, along with some indecisiveness at times. Both Mr. Spoon and Ms. Fork are the same age but need healing and deliverance in their character flaws as individuals. Neither one will receive healing on the same day. It may take one a little longer to reach their potential, and it may take the other a little less time to reach theirs. God looks at the individual person, not that the age. God meets that person where they are spiritually and begins there. Once they overcome even the tiniest deficiencies that have been problematic for their spiritual growth in their own time, God graduates them to the next level... they will "level up" in their spirit man. There's no "at the end" commencement speech. God does not hold His applause to the end of the year. He gives you kudos each time you come up a bit higher in Him. He gives you a spiritual diploma in *every* growth in Him.

So, let's graduate in Christ. Let's "level up!" Go before Christ and ask Him to show you things about ourselves that you need to grow away from, things that may be hindering your spiritual journey. Remember, we will never be perfect, but we can be more mature in Him. Now is the time to "level up!"

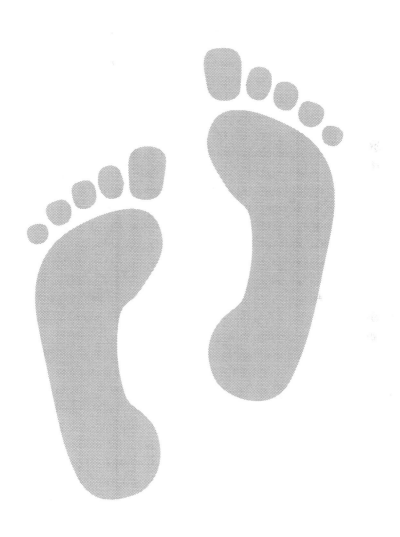

Chapter 27
COMMUNING WITH GOD IN THE NIGHT

Sometimes, when you are in darkness, it can be a time for zoning out all of your distractions and focusing on the only light that is in your view. It can be a time for healing or a time for reflecting without all of the daily busy things that you have to deal with on a regular basis. Silence in the night is not necessarily a bad thing when it is God who is allowing the tranquility to happen so we can see Him, His light in the dark. "The light shines in the darkness, and the darkness has not overcome" (NIV, John 1.5).

Peace can represent being still, being silent. Darkness can represent tuning out all the noise that occurs in your life and focusing on that still small voice of God. Sometimes, God wakes people up early in the wee hours of the morning to commune with Him. Why, because it's mostly quiet during the night. People had already ran errands, prepared dinner, most activities have ceased, kids are in bed possibly waiting on school the following day, and parents are in bed sleeping waiting for the next workday to begin. It is the perfect time of the night when you can hear the stillness of your own feet creaking the floorboards as you walk, or you can hear the crickets chirping against the moonlight. Silence (when God's initiating it) is good for our growth when we allow it. There's no fear in this kind of darkness, only peace, and tranquility.

Focus on the light to get your mind centered.

Focus on the light to get your mind in unity with God's thoughts.

Focus on the light to get your mind, body, and soul aligned with God's Will. Allow the light to illuminate the things that are pertinent to God's heart for you. "Your word *is* a lamp to my feet, And a light to my path" (NKJV, Psalms 119.105).

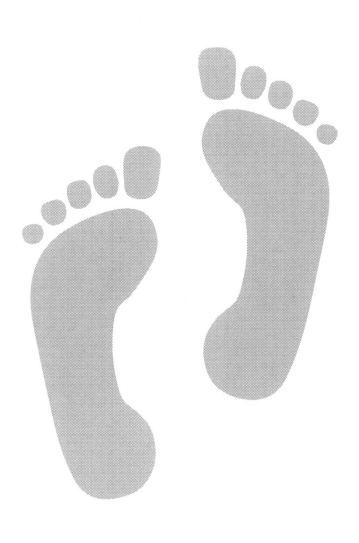

Chapter 28
I MISS YOU

I Miss You!

I miss my dad on a regular basis, and he has been deceased for over 20 years now. I believe you are entitled to miss your loved ones for eternity. There is no time frame that says, "enough is enough." I remember my ex-husband, during the marriage, said to me after two weeks of grieving over my dad's death, that I should be over him by now. I married young at the time, and he did not know how to handle or comfort someone that was experiencing a death of a loved one. I did not fault him for his lack of understanding. I basically sucked it up, and later after we had divorced, God taught me that grieving was ok; it was healthy for me. The trick was **not** to allow grieving to paralyze me. Sometimes, when we grieve hard for someone, it can be so overwhelming that we can drown in it. This can prevent us from maintaining a job, relationships, health, and completing our day-to-day functions (cooking, cleaning, driving a car, etc.). Grieving can paralyze us if we are deeply broken-hearted over our loved ones.

God can help us remember the memories without their death consuming us. This is when we can rely on God's strength to keep us afloat, so we don't drown in our sorrows. His strength is so much bigger than we can ever imagine. "My grace is sufficient for you, for My strength is made perfect in weakness" (NIV, 2 Corinthians 12.9). His strength *is* made perfect our weakness!

Imagine King Kong (from the movies) gently holding you in his huge hand, and you do not have the strength to move from your grieving spot. When you rest yourself in the hands of God, which is much bigger than the hands of King Kong, He will provide that strength you need. His hand will lift you up from that "stuck spot" of despair and assist you in moving forward in your life if you let Him. "Do not fear, for I am with you; do not be afraid, for I am your God. I will strengthen you; I will help you; I will hold on to you with My righteous right hand" (NIV, Isaiah 41.10). When you grieve, first pray and ask God to take control of your grieving process. Ask God to never allow yourself to grieve beyond your capabilities of functioning in your day-to-day life. This allows God to help you to mourn without it consuming you. Believe that God is going to do what you prayed for.

Grief allows those wonderful memories to flow through your eyes in tears with God as your tissue.

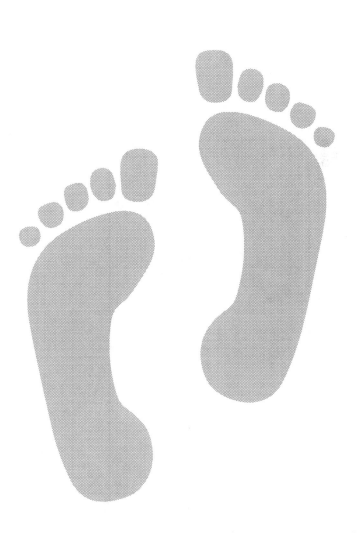

Chapter 29
THE HOLY SPIRIT ILLUMINATES YOU

What is the Holy Spirit? Who is the Holy Spirit?

The Holy Spirit is an extension of God. He is a person. The Holy Spirit comforts us when we need Him. He gives us the peace we need in difficult times. The Holy Spirit resonates in every believer of Christ. He helps you to fight the enemy more efficiently, and He covers you when you are sincerely trying to please Christ. The Spirit of God, who *is* alive, actuates *in you* that God is alive. He reminds you that God is real. The Word of God is alive because of the Holy Spirit who dwells in the Living Word of God.

This is what I believe happens when we read the Word of God:

When we open the Bible to engage in it, The Holy Spirit in us connects with The Holy Spirit in the Word of God, and the Holy Spirit starts downloading things into our spirit. There's a transference that happens from our spirit to the Word and from the Word of God to our spirit. We may not always understand fully what we read, but it is ok. The Holy Spirit will download into your spirit what He wants you to know. As you witness to someone, the Holy Spirit will give you something you needed to be more effective in your witnessing even if you didn't quite understand what you were reading in your earlier devotion. It's a supernatural phenomenon that is not always understood by man. "And the Spirit of the LORD shall rest upon him, the Spirit of wisdom and understanding, the Spirit of counsel and might, the Spirit of knowledge and the fear of the LORD" (ESV, Isaiah 11.2).

God works with His disciples of Christ, who can understand His Word with all readiness. And God also works with those disciples whose hearts are right but struggle to understand the things they are learning in His Word. God is no respecter of person. He meets you where you are and help you in your learning style. It is truly a remarkable thing. "But the Helper, the Holy Spirit, whom the Father will send in my name, he will teach you all things and bring to your remembrance all that I have said to you" (ESV, John 14.26).

When we trust God and allow the Holy Spirit to dwell in us, we can become more peaceful as our confidence increases in knowing that He can fill us with His presence in our relationship with Him.

The Holy Spirit is also in every form of Worship, including prayer. I absolutely love it when I pray with fervency, and I can feel The Holy Spirit resting on my prayers. At times, I feel like I'm in a beautifully decorated place where it is just me, God, and The Holy Spirit. There's so much peace when I get to this place in prayer. This also happens when I sing psalms unto the Lord. I feel The Holy Spirit in my worship. I feel light, elevated, and at peace in my worship. I love it when the Holy Spirit rests in my worship. It is an awesome experience.

So, in your worship, in your prayer life, or even in your devotion, allow The Holy Spirit to illuminate Himself in you; it's a beautiful connection.

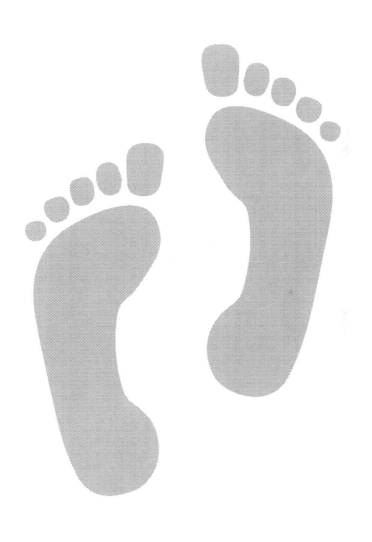

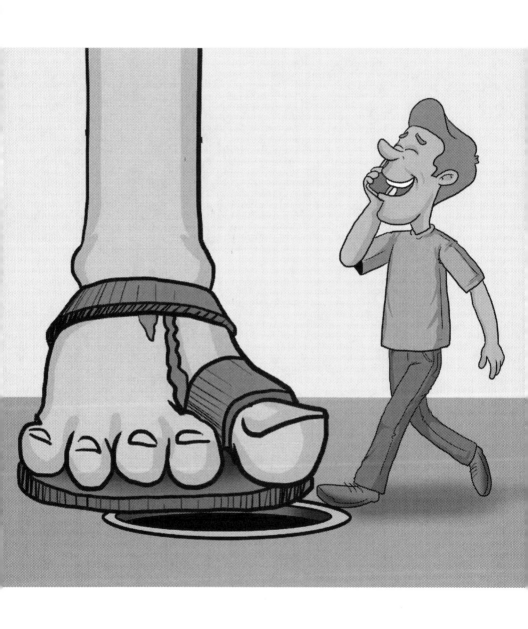

Chapter 30
DISTRACTIONS

Distractions can be dangerous when it takes away from listening and obeying God. Many things in life that will lead us away from God's Will if we are not careful. We must not give into those interruptions. God's plan for us comes with an individual pathway that we should follow to reach our destiny. "For I know the plans I have for you," declares the Lord, "plans to prosper you and not to harm you, plans to give you hope and a future" (NIV, Jeremiah 29.11).

The enemy has an agenda to distract God's Chosen people. The adversary wants to divert or delay the objectives Christ has in place for you. If the enemy can tempt us with something that is unhealthy to our spirit, that leads us away from the Will of God, then it is a distraction. For instance, God may have a spouse in mind for you, but if you are not willing to let go of the unhealthy relationship you are in now, you end up settling for less than God's best. Your decision to remain in that "wrong relationship" hinders the outcome for your future. Remember, the enemy loves sending counterfeit relationships to distract you.

God may be calling you to go higher in Him, but your unwillingness to prepare delays God's provision for you and it becomes a "win-win" for the enemy. If the enemy can keep you off course, he is keeping you less effective in the kingdom of God. The enemy has nullified your God given power.

Distractions takes your focus off of Christ:

For instance, binge watching too many shows on Netflix throughout the week instead of creating time to draw closer to Christ can be a diversion. It keeps you tapped into something else rather than God. Distractions keeps you drawn into the world it has created for you instead of being led into the spiritual world that Christ has created for you.

Distractions can hinder God's plan:

The children of Israel were on an eleven-day trip but it took them 40 years to reach their destination (KJV, Deuteronomy 1-2). Because of their rebelliousness, God didn't allow them to cross over the Jordan River into the Promise Land. He allowed the NEXT generation to see the Promise Land. I believe when we allow interruptions to interfere with our destiny in Christ, we take a chance in permanently delaying our future because of how comfortable we choose to be in the wilderness. So, let's pack our bags and move FORWARD into our God-given destiny.

Distractions can cause us to settle:

You have been working at a job that has no advancements in moving up in the company. There's another job that offers many opportunities to excel further with better benefits in the company, but you would rather settle where you are at. You say to yourself, "I already know this job inside and out." Or "I don't want the hassle of learning something new," but it may be God's divine plan for you to invest in a better company to get the blessings you deserve. But instead, we settle for what God didn't intend for our future, which bring more financial problems and hardships because we avoided the opportunities to be in a better place. God wants the best for us, but when we don't want the best for ourselves, we tie God's hands, and that ties our future in having more. Take the opportunity!

Distractions are there to keep us from doing the will of God:

A busybody person can accomplish a lot in a day and still come up short in their efforts to maintain their relationship with God. You can always be there for other people but neglect the alone time you need to regenerate your spirit in the presence of God. Christ may have put someone on your mind for you to reach out to with a card, a phone call, or a visit, but you keep allowing other distractions to entertain you. Soon that thought has faded from your mind, and you forget altogether what you were supposed to have done for God. Let God use you to be a blessing to others.

Distractions are there to keep us occupied with unnecessary things:

Let's say you are supposed to start a Bible study in your home to witness the Word of God to others. Instead, you tell yourself you want to finish the (unimportant) projects you have been meaning to get to first. Distractions can snowball into other things. Once you finally get done with your unimportant projects, your mind naturally creates other things to do afterwards. The cycle of diversion continues over and over as the desire to please God vanishes from your spirit. It is time to break the cycle!

Distractions can lead you to compromise your standards and hinder your salvation:

We Christians can get caught up in altering our biblical principles and standards to please people or ingratiating ourselves in a world that is not our own. It is like the guards that position themselves at the Tower of London, which are called Yeoman Warders. They are upholding a standard that they dare not deviate from. Even when someone tries to distract them, they are immoveable abiding by the laws and rules they follow. We as Christians can be distracted by allowing little things that can filter into our standards and principles, causing us to compromise God's Will for our lives, and we stumble and fall in our walk with Christ. Become immoveable!

Distractions can lead you into the wrong life:

Associating with the wrong group of people can diminish your Christian spirit. Their toxic spirit can cause you to end up in the wrong life that was not meant for you. In your desperation, you settle into a risky lifestyle that is contrary to the one God had planned for you.

Stay fixed on God's mission and provisions for your life. Look up and stay focused!

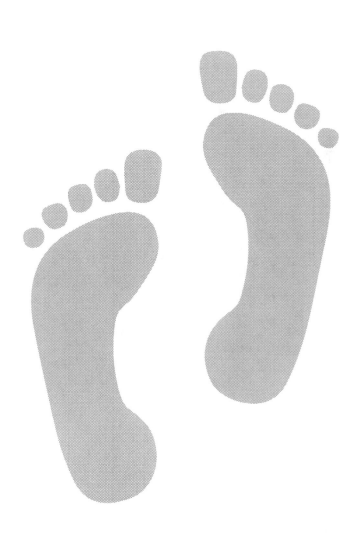

Chapter 31
PAY THE BILL BEFORE THE LIGHT GETS CUT OFF

In the above chapter title, notice there's no "s" in the word light. That is not an error. It was intentional. That's because I'm referring to your spiritual light. The spiritual light that God gives us all when we accept His salvation. It's like a candle we have been given when we accept Jesus Christ into our lives. It's automatically given to us, lit. We just have to keep it **lit** daily as we walk out our Christian life.

Salvation is free. Jesus died on the cross for our sins. Jesus paid the penalty for us to live free in Him. So, when it comes to salvation, there is no bill that needs to be paid.

So, what do I mean when I say "pay the bill before the light gets cut off?" I am referring to your spiritual sacrifice. Our light can dim when we spend less time with God on a regular basis. Our light can go out when we don't spend time in prayer...or in the Word...or in Worship.

Most of us faith believers wouldn't intentionally allow our light to get cut off. God allows us to see better spiritually when we cultivate and strengthen our relationship with Him. We can **see** what we are doing more succinctly. We can **see** the direction we are going into with clarity. We can **see** the enemy's tactics clearer. We can **see** the next step we are taking when we keep the light on.

When we don't invest in God, we end up spiritually depleted, and our light is extinguished. Then, when we realize we can't see without God, we try to feel our way back. When the light is off, you only see darkness, and you can't see how **close** God is to you. The longer you stay in the dark, the more the enemy will make you feel worthless, as if we don't deserve having the light on. The enemy will make you feel valueless through doubt, shame, insecurities, and depression, ultimately keeping you further away from the light of God. Your spiritual strength to reconnect to weakened by the enemy's stumbling blocks. The enemy will also have you feeling like you have to jump through hoops to get your light back on, but that's not true.

God like is a Motel 6. He leaves the light on for you." God says "Come to me, all you who are weary and burdened, and I will give you rest. Take my yoke upon you and learn from me, for I am gentle and humble in heart, and you will find rest for your souls. For my yoke is easy, and my burden is light" (NIV, Matthew 11.28-30).

So, run full speed into God's arms! It is just that easy! Go before God, truly repent, and ask for forgiveness! As long as you have breath in your body, it will always be that easy! Don't let the enemy fool you! Keep your light on!

Once we have reconnected the light of God, we **see** that He was right before us the *entire time.*

So, pay the bill with your sacrifice to God to keep your light shining bright like a diamond because you cannot afford to have your light turned off!

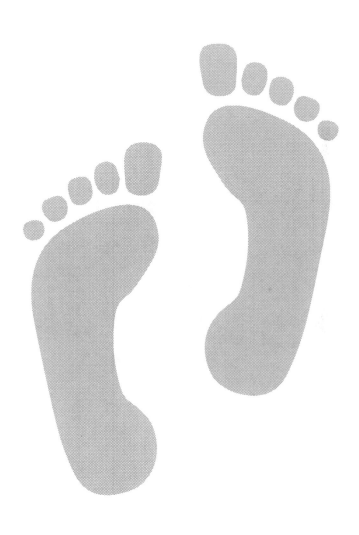

Chapter 32
JOINING THE CHURCH

Picking a church to attend on a regular basis is a lot like buying a house. There's a lot to think about: is it small/big enough for me? Is there a daycare or children's church if I have children? Does the church receive me with a warm welcome? Are they consistently caring about me after I have joined? Does the church offer spiritual counseling if I need it? Does the church offer various spiritual classes to strengthen my spirit and to keep me growing in God? Are there ways to serve in the church? Do they have outreach programs that I can be a part of? Are the sermons strong enough to carry me through trials and tests? Does the spoken Word of God make me a better believer and disciple for Christ? Does God's Word agree with the spoken word in that church?

There are so many things to consider before committing to a church. I found several things to consider in the very beginning that will help you in your quest in choose a church more smoothly.

First of all, pray. "Do not be anxious about anything, but in every situation, by prayer and petition, with thanksgiving, present your requests to God. And the peace of God, which transcends all understanding, will guard your hearts and your minds in Christ Jesus" (NIV, Philippians 4.6-7). Pray about every church you attend as a guest to see if it is the church that God wants you to fellowship at. Allow God to have the final word over every decision you make to ensure that you are attending the right church that will help you grow and mature in your walk with Christ. Through God's peace, you will know the church is the right fit for you.

Secondly, THERE IS NO PERFECT CHURCH. I repeat, THERE IS NO PERFECT CHURCH. I cannot stress this enough. "For all have sinned and fall short of the glory of God" (NIV, Romans 3.23). NO church is perfect, so walk into every church building with that mindset to keep your rigid expectations to a minimum. Just like a house you choose to buy, you may have things you didn't expect that may come up or neighbors that you didn't think had character flaws. You might have found the right house but have to deal with the loud and obnoxious neighbor that lives next to you. You might have to deal with the neighbor who thinks everyone should cut their grass when he thinks it should be cut. There's a lot of character flaws in all of us believers because we are STILL human. The Bible is FULL of people who walked with God but STILL had proclivities. You have character flaws too. I have character flaws. I believe God designed it that way to help all of us deal with each other's character flaws respectfully and in love. So please keep that in mind.

Thirdly, if God has given you the green light to make that church your home, stay planted until He tells you to move. The longer we attend a church, the more we are subjected to see or hear things that may rub us the wrong way. If we don't have a thick skin, it may cause us to leave prematurely. I believe God uses other believers to buffer us sometimes. He uses other believers to make us stronger in our walk with Him.

If your spirit disagrees with something you witnessed, heard, or saw in the church, it doesn't mean you go along with it. It just means you are going to maintain your salvation by taking it to the Lord and asking *Him* how to deal with what you had witnessed, heard or saw. It doesn't necessarily mean you are going to find another church (unless God has CLEARLY spoken to you about leaving).

Offenses can be difficult at times. In the Oxford Dictionary, offenses mean annoyance or resentment brought about by a perceived insult to or disregard for oneself or one's standards or principles. If you can build a backbone with most offenses and allow God to direct your steps on how to handle those offenses instead of allowing your flesh and emotions to uproot you, then you are going to be much wiser in your walk with the Lord. Honor God in the midst of chaos. Honor God until He tells you to leave the church. Show your strength by walking through it unaffected, unharmed, while God makes **you** stronger *through* it.

Church is just like a sport's team in some ways. You have one goal, and that is to win for the team (winning souls for Christ). You all are on the same team (same faith), with the same coach (the pastor), learning the same schematic that teaches you how to get to the finish line (schematic that keep you growing in God). If a player on the team is not taking things seriously (a believer in Christ), that's ok, just make sure **you** are taking your salvation seriously. You are the one that is going to get ahead in the spiritual realm. People around you will see your strength by the way you handle circumstances. Your faith in God will be a light to others. Your strength to overcome is in Him, and that allows you to understand how to deal with people's character flaws without quickly running away. If you decide to become a runner, you may become a permanent runner and never building roots or growth because you couldn't deal with a few character flaws in church people. Don't run but fight through it with the help of the Lord until God releases you.

Church people are just like your own brothers and sisters: There may be some bickering between two members. They are just like family members. There may be one that is an amazing cook, another one that likes to gossip about others, and another one who confesses to be saved but still sins on weekend. They are just like your neighbors or your co-workers. Church people are just saved through God's grace and mercy, and just like the disciples in the Bible, we all still have to get along to carry out God's great commission.

So, ask God to help you find a church so you can stay planted and grow through tribulations and trials.

In the end, *you* may end up being the change that is needed in that church.

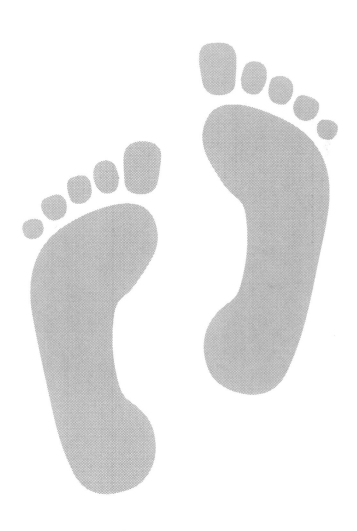

Chapter 33
DEDICATED TO GOD

Bishop, author, and filmmaker TD Jakes said something so profound. He said, "I'd rather serve God as if there *is* a God than to not serve God and find out there was a God."

There are many things people do to hear God. Someone may "fast" (which is a type of sacrament that is done unto the Lord), another may commit to Eucharist prayers, and another may use liturgical music to worship the Lord. Some people pray over their house, and others anoint their forehead with holy oil in an attempt to get connected to God. "So, whether we are at home or away, we make it our aim to please him" (NIV, 2 Corinthians 5.9).

God is pleased with anything you do to connect yourself to His spirit. Every sacrifice you make in the flesh builds spiritual strength. Since the devil doesn't play fair, we need to be sharp and alert spiritually so we can have a better chance of winning battles in our mind and flesh.

Some people may judge you and say, "it does not take all of that to reach God," but guess what, your spiritual path is different from someone else's. You are on your own spiritual journey, and God is directing *your* path in this Christian walk. We are all striving to honor, worship, and to be a servant in Christ. I believe God honors what *you* do for Him. What works for you may not work for others. What works for others may not work for you. God rewards *your* efforts either covertly or through inner growth.

In the Bible, the woman did everything she could to get to Jesus. She was trying to touch the hem of His garment. When she did, she was free from her burden, and when you do, you keep yourself free from being tangled in bondage (KJV, John 4.1-42).

Other people may not understand the level of sacrifice you are making to hear from The Lord. That sacrifice keeps you communing and connected to God. Others can make you feel that it doesn't take that much sacrifice, but it does for *you*, and God is *pleased* with any effort you give Him. You are saying, "I love you Lord. I want to stay in your presence."

It doesn't matter what you have to do to stay connected to The Almighty God. Just keep doing it!

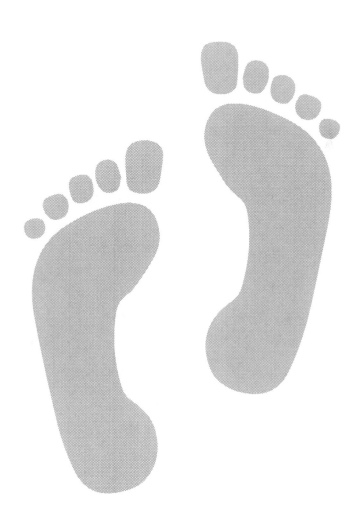

Chapter 34
GOD LOVES YOUR UNIQUENESS

God loves each and every one of us.

People are yellow, black, white, red, brown, tan, and any combination of any colors. We are ALL precious in His sight. Jesus loves ALL the children of the world, no matter how old we are. From birth to over 100 years old, we will always be God's children. Why? Because He loves what He creates, every single human that is breathing. God loves how He formed and fashioned you. He sprinkled you with uniqueness, that makes you skillfully different from someone else. We are all flawless to Him. God does not have an issue with your skin tone or your eccentric style. He doesn't have a problem with our deformities, disposition, birth defects, proclivities, mental issues, or physical impairments. "I will praise thee; for I am fearfully and wonderfully made: marvelous are thy works; and that my soul knoweth right well" (KJV, Psalms 139.14).

I believe God has an issue with sin that *we* create through our physical, mental, or temperament. For instance, you may have a birth defect that you are not fond of, and instead of asking God to change your perspective about how you feel about your birth defect, you decide to minimize others through negative words that hurt instead of words that heal. Sometimes, we may need to first ask God how to love ourselves so that we can love others.

As children of The Most High God, we need to simulate, emulate, and implement His love for others. We need to see people the way

God sees people. It is essential that we adopt God's spirit in loving others.

There are people that can be exasperating or difficult to love, but God can show *you,* how to show them love when we petition to God for His aid.

In this current world, we see too much hate and abuse. My Bishop Ronald Logan, once told me that hurting people hurt other people. That has always stuck with me. So, when we see someone physically, mentally, or spiritually abusing someone about their gender, ethnicity, race, height, weight, deformities, etc., it is a result of someone negatively impacting their own lives in some way, and they are dishing that negativity out to others. When you peel back the layers and get to the core root of their problem, you will see someone who is responding or teaching out of hurt or pain. Someone may be too toxic for *you* to deal with, and God may be trying to keep *you* safe and out of harm's way. A close relationship with God helps us to determine if we need to love someone from a safe distance if that ends up being the case, or how to love someone who is carries a negative spirit.

But in general, every one of us is eccentric in some way. God didn't make everyone the same. He made everyone as unique as possible. Even identical twins are unique is some ways. DNA is unique. That's why we have hundreds of different colors, sizes, and shapes of people. God designed us this way.

Let's leave our judgmental thoughts in God's hands and focus on showing God's love to others so that God can get the glory out of your life.

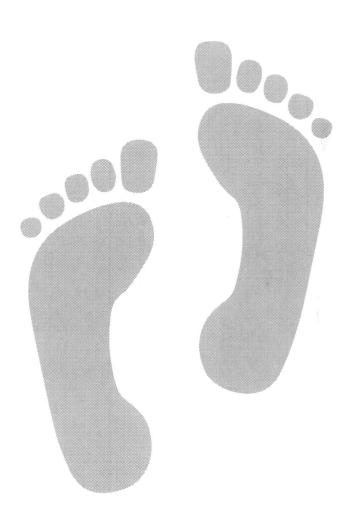

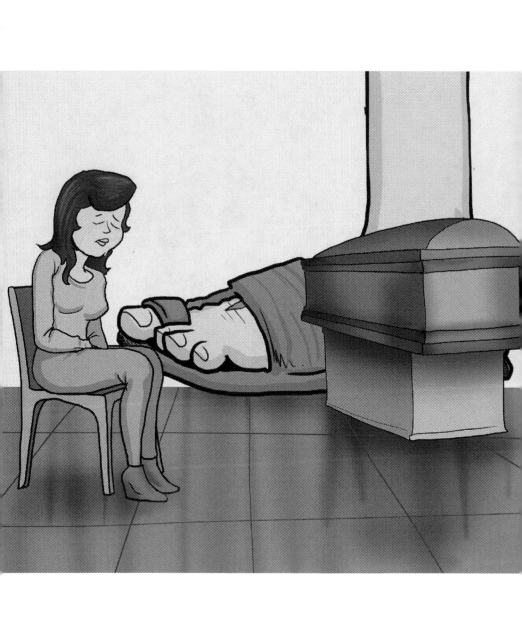

Chapter 35
LET THE RELATIONSHIP DIE

One of the most difficult parts of a funeral (and I had witnessed this with my own father's death) is when the lid of the casket closes. For some reason, when I saw the lid close, I cried more. I grieved more. I knew it was over. I knew I would never see my dad's face again.

When we walk away from toxic relationships or bad friendships, it can feel just like we are at a funeral and mourning the relationship. It can be hard to let go.

Some of us may have walked away multiple times from that same toxic relationship/friendship, but we keep going back because we haven't closed the lid (the final piece) in an effort to finalize the end of the relationship.

The open lid can represent reliving memories, remembering the good times, and forgetting about how unhealthy it was. By leaving the lid up on the casket, we are saying, "I know it's over, but I'm not ready. I know I have to walk away. I know I have to leave this unhealthy relationship, but it's hard."

In the relationship, you probably spent a lot of time with that person. You probably had some bright moments, but nothing outweighs how harmful it has been overall. Your emotions only want to see the good, but your common sense knows that the right thing to do is to leave.

Put the lid down once and for all on that toxic relationship. Yes, it will hurt. Yes, you will probably cry more, but allow that relationship to **die**. Allow God to deal with your emotional roller coaster of feelings. Let God help you to control your emotions so you can bury that unhealthy relationship. At this point, you may need God to fill you with His strength so you can overcome this situation. "The LORD is my strength and my defense; he has become my salvation. He is my God, and I will praise him, my father's God, and I will exalt Him" (NIV, Exodus 15.2).

I remember being in a toxic relationship. When I walked away, he became my stalker for over a year. I didn't know what to do initially when he started stalking me, but I went to God. I sought God for help and protection. God told me what to do step by step, day by day, but I had to do it God's way for total freedom. Every day, I would wake up and ask God what do I do today as I prayed for His covering, peace, and freedom. Eventually, the frequency became less and less until he ceased stalking me completely. I know every situation is different, but God *does* have the right strategy for us if we are ready to walk away from things that are dangerous to our future. "Look to the LORD and his strength; seek his face always" (NIV, 1 Chronicles 16.11).

Sometimes, our insecurities keep us in an unhealthy situation. Our unhealthy insecurities (which is part of our soul) marries the other person's unhealthy insecurities before our flesh does at times, creating a soul tie. Did you catch that? We attract who we are. If we are feeling unworthy in our spirit, we attract a mate who is feeling the same way long before we actually walk down the aisle in marriage with them.

We long for someone to accept our flaws or insecurities. When we have someone that accepts our proclivities, we sometimes ignore the major red flags, such as mental or physical abuse issues in the other person. This can create a false acceptance in one another based on fear or selfish desires instead of a good foundation. For instance, one person's jealousy in the relationship may prevent the other person from advancing in a job career because the person is afraid that he/she will leave them. In another relationship, someone may feel they can stray from the relationship and know that other will eventually take them back over and over because of insecurities or fear of being alone. Our insecurities won't let us believe we deserve better or that God will give us better. We may simply be tired of waiting for better and would rather have what we accepted. Allow God to heal what is broken inside of your spirit and soul so you can understand you deserve more.

Sometimes in life, due to our situations, background, culture, or learned behaviors, we grow up believing something negative. A lie may have been spoken into us that we carry in our minds for many years. God can fill us with His spirit to strengthen us so it can transform us into a person with standards, self-love, and a desire for God's best. "So do not fear, for I am with you; do not be dismayed, for I am your God. I will strengthen you and help you; I will uphold you with my righteous right hand" (NIV, Isaiah 41.10).

So, close the casket lid and let that toxic relationship die once and for all!

Chapter 36
KICK THE HABIT

An addiction is anything that keeps us wanting more. It is a dependency on something. It is something we can't seem to live without. It can be a drug, food, alcohol, clothes, objects, or even a person or activity. It can end up controlling our lives to the point where it can be harmful to our health, finances, or mentality. An addiction can become a necessity or a craving. It can get to the point where our mind no longer wants it, but our body craves it. It no longer becomes a decision to choose but an automatic activation in the body that overrides the mind's decision to stop. Sometimes, the absence of not having the thing we crave can cause our body to go into shock or withdrawals.

God can either deliver someone from an addiction instantly or sometimes, He allows us to go through a process. In the process, it may take work through fervent prayer, medication, programs, treatment, using abstinence, etc. During this time, I believe God wants us to walk it out by walking through it so that we can teach others how to be set free from the same addiction. We become a testimony.

We never know which method God is going to dispense His deliverance through, but we should petition to God in prayer about our concerns and trust His plan of action for our individual lives.

Being addicted to something can create an idol in our spirit. An idol is anything that takes precedence over God. It's anything that holds or occupies our attention more than our obedience in Christ.

Here are some questions that you need to ask yourself:

Can you go without it?

Do you have to have it on a regular basis?

Are you drawn to it when stress, trauma, or depression occurs in your life?

Has it interfered with your day to day living?

Has it caused financial woes?

Do you experience cravings or withdrawals when you feel you need to stop?

If you answered yes to any of these, then seek God and ask Him to reveal to you how you can gain more self-control over the situation.

God never wants anything that can consume us, hurt us, or affect us in the long run.

Too much of a good thing can cause potential harm to our mental or physical state. Some people end up with high cholesterol, high blood pressure, diabetes, heart problems, addiction problems, etc. Too much of a good thing or in the wrong context crosses over into sinful pleasures when we don't exercise self-control in eliminating things that harm God's temple, if you are a child of God.

1 John 2:16 "For everything in the world–the lust of the flesh, the lust of the eyes, and the pride of life–comes not from the Father but from the world." (New International Version) NIV

James 4:7 "Submit yourselves, then, to God. Resist the devil, and he will flee from you." (New International Version) NIV

Titus 2:12 teaches us to say "No" to ungodliness and worldly passions, and to live self-controlled, upright and godly lives in this present age…" (New International Version) NIV

Let God help you fight the battle of addiction that has consumed your mind and body. You **can** overcome it. God says that you can if you believe it. "Ye are of God, little children, and have **overcome** them: because greater is He that is in **you**, than he that is in the world" (NIV,1 John 4.4).

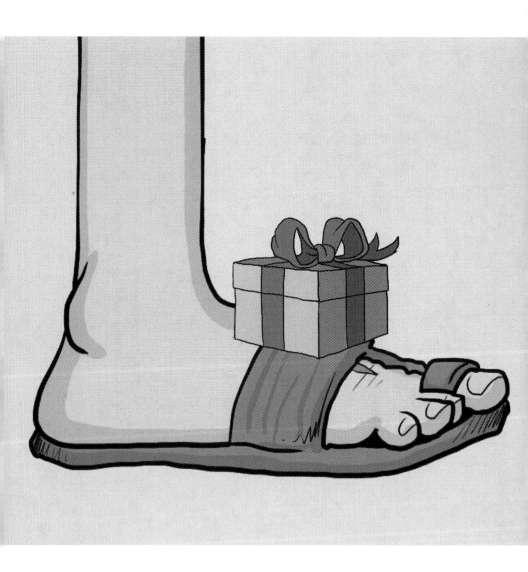

Chapter 37
GIFT OF GOD: JOHN 3:16

What is the Meaning of the Cross?

The Gift of God represents having propitiation for our sins. If Jesus had not died for our sins, there would be no forgiveness for our sins, and we would be in damnation for the rest of our lives. The enemy would have had an easy win over our souls, but since God gave us His only begotten Son, we have remission for our sins. We have someone that is giving us another choice. Someone that can remove our sins, our hurt, our pain, our suffering and replace it with His peace, His comfort, and His love. It is the feeling you get when you are free from the entrapment of sin or addiction. The enemy is not capable of giving us the freedom we need.

Imagine a rain cloud over our heads everywhere we go. We could never get away from it. It would follow us into our homes, into our cars, on the job, and anywhere else we would go. It would be constantly pouring down rain on us metaphorically in the spirit. No way out. We could not get cleaned or dry. We would be constantly soaked in sin…day and night.

Now, we have a way out. Now, we can call on our Lord Jesus Christ to stop the rain and the soaking. God stepped up and said I will give you a choice to be dry. You do not have to be soaked and wet anymore. God's salvation dries us off when we chose Him. God's salvation gives us that ability to keep dry from colds, flu, shivering, etc., when we chose Him (metaphorically).

Why? Because our Lord Jesus Christ *loves* us so much. His love is so big that it is unconditional, which is beyond human's capacity to love. God goes beyond our human ability to love. People love parts and pieces of us. They love what they like or their connection to us. Jesus loves EVERY part of you. The parts that you like and the parts that you don't like. The parts that you try to hide and the parts that you are ashamed of. Jesus loves the hidden truth about you. Jesus embraces your failures and your mistakes. He embraces your scars and your bad habits.

Jesus sacrificed Himself on the cross for YOU. "For God so loved the world that he gave his one and only Son, that whoever believes in him shall not perish but have eternal life" (NIV, John 3.16). YOU matter to Jesus. Your life, your direction, your future matter to our Lord Jesus Christ.

God's gift and love for you is His one and only son, Jesus Christ.

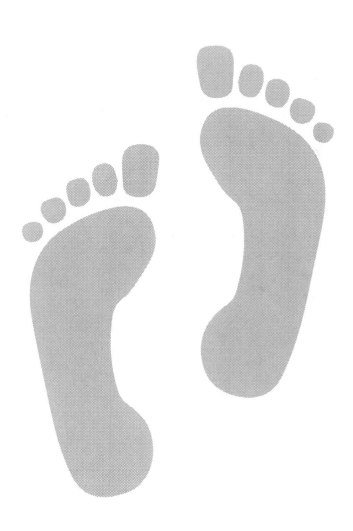

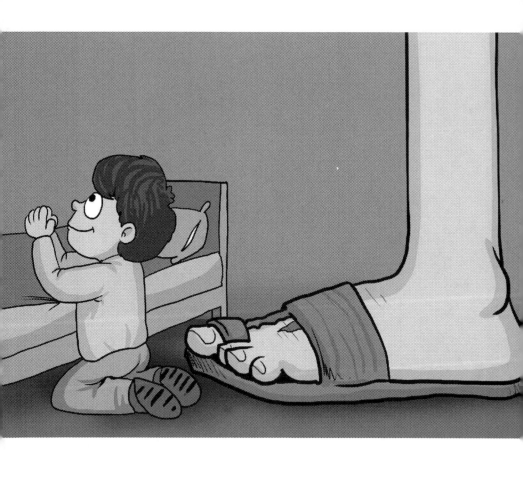

Chapter 38
THE LORD'S PRAYER

"After this manner therefore pray ye: Our Father which art in heaven, Hallowed be thy name. Thy kingdom come. Thy will be done in earth, as it is in heaven. Give us this day our daily bread. And forgive us our debts, as we forgive our debtors. And lead us not into temptation, but deliver us from evil: For thine is the kingdom, and the power, and the glory, forever. Amen" (KJV, Matthew 6.9-13).

Meaning Of The Lord's Prayer

Verse 9: *Our Father which art in heaven, Hallowed be thy name:* This is referring to the one and only Father who sits on the throne in the heaven of heavenlies. He created the universe; everything above, below and in the earth (KJV, Genesis 1). Holy is His name because the Lord is the most genuine, authentic, unequivocal, perfect love there is. Our Father has perfected the "unconditional love" he has for all of us.

Verse 10. *Thy kingdom come. Thy will be done in earth, as it is in heaven:* The Lord has a kingdom that will take the place of this earth one day. It *is* coming! He has already set *in* the earth the day, time, and hour of when this will happen. The Lord alone knows. Our job is to stay "woke" just like the 5 wise virgins in the bible (KJV, Matthew 25.1-13). We do not know the day, time, or hour of when we are going to take our last breath here on earth. Be wise enough not to take your next breath for granted. Stay ready for the kingdom to come.

Verse 11. *Give us this day our daily bread:* I believe this verse is referring to spiritual food that sustains us. We need spiritual food daily to nourish the soul, to feed the mind and to give us the energy to "walk" in God's Will.

Verse 12. *And forgive us our debts, as we forgive our debtors:* You may have heard the saying "what comes around, goes around" or "do unto others as you would have them done unto you." If the Lord forgives us, we need to be able to forgive others. When your hands are holding onto unforgiveness or grudges, you have no room to receive or catch your blessings.

Verse 13. *And lead us not into temptation, but deliver us from evil:* I interpret this as a plead for covering against the adversary. The verse acknowledges that temptation is inevitable. Because we know this in advance, we can call on the name of Lord to gives us a way of escape from the temptation.

Verse 13, Conclusion. *For thine is the kingdom, and the power, and the glory, forever. Amen:* We give reverence to our Lord and Savior, Jesus Christ. We acknowledge that He has the whole world in his hands.

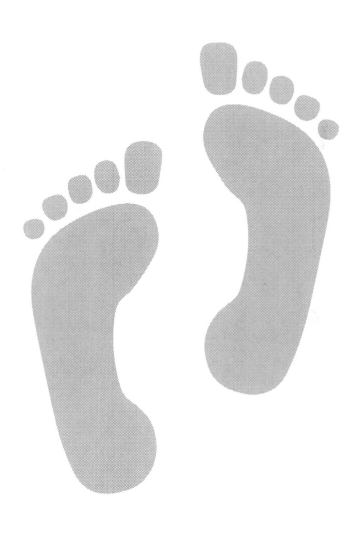

Chapter 39
RECEIVING SALVATION

Are you ready to receive our Lord Jesus Christ as your Savior? Are you ready to allow God to transform your life so you can start living in freedom? Say the Salvation Prayer below with an open and readiness heart and your sins will be washed away into the sea of forgetfulness. "He will turn again, he will have compassion upon us; he will subdue our iniquities; and thou wilt cast all their sins into the depths of the sea" (KJV, Micah 7.19).

Salvation Prayer

Heavenly Father, I come to you in the name of Jesus. I acknowledge to You that I am a sinner, and I am sorry for my sins and the life that I have lived; I need your forgiveness. I believe with all my heart that you Lord Jesus Christ died on the cross for my sake and has risen from the dead. You said in your Holy Word "That if thou shalt confess with thy mouth the Lord Jesus, and shalt believe in thine heart that God hath raised him from the dead, thou shalt be saved" (KJV, Romans 10.9). Lord I receive your Word, and I repent of my sins, I renounce my past. Lord Jesus Christ come into my heart; I receive my forgiveness. I receive the new birth, cleansed and washed in the Word and in the precious blood of Jesus. Fill me with your Spirit, in Jesus' name, Amen!

Printed in the United States
by Baker & Taylor Publisher Services